The Ministry of Listening

The Ministry of Listening

Team Visiting in Hospital and Home

Donald Peel

Anglican Book Centre
Toronto, Canada

Printed in Canada
ISBN 0-919030-57-2

Typesetting & Art
New Line Graphics Ltd.

to Alice who visited me

Contents

Preface

This book is for lay people who minister to others. It focuses on hospital visiting, but it will introduce you to many kinds of helping ministry. People are people, wherever they are. Their needs are the same, and the ways of helping them are similar. The basic technique is creative listening. The principles of creative listening apply not only to hospital visiting, but also to visiting the elderly in seniors' residences or nursing homes, shut-ins in their houses, housebound young mothers, distressed companions in the work force, needy neighbors across the back fence, parents of your Sunday school pupils, newcomers to your congregation – anyone with whom you intentionally engage in helpful conversation. This book will help you minister to people at their point of greatest felt need. It draws on the accumulated knowledge of the social sciences and is based on biblical principles.

The number of people needing help in our society is enormous. The opportunity for caring ministry is limitless, and it is something lay persons often do best. If you feel the call to be a lay visitor, this book can help you. By its description of and teaching about hospital ministry, it will give you an idea of what all pastoral ministry is like. You may learn, however, that this ministry is not for you, that your sphere of Christian service lies elsewhere than in an intensive, specialized, personal ministry. That will be all to the good. It won't mean that you're uninterested in ministry. Interest is one thing and calling another. In this book you'll find out what pastoral visitors do. Then you'll be able to support the people who do have the calling. You can pray for them and help the church provide for the formation of lay visiting teams.

A tremendous opportunity exists, especially in hospitals, for Christians with proper training to witness to the love and power of Christ. The magnitude of this opportunity becomes apparent when it is realized that more people pass through the nation's hospitals than through any other institution in our society. People in times of sickness often find themselves pondering the meaning of life, inwardly searching for answers, for peace, for wholeness, for God.

Some of them cling desperately to a vague faith and reach out for more. Others ransack their memories for ultimate reality among the discarded fragments of a long-neglected faith. People like these can be found everywhere. But it is the sick in hospital who have an abundance of time to think and are often happy to have someone to talk to, someone who will try to understand them, accept them, and minister to them "where they are." They need listeners with an accurate feel for what they consciously or unconsciously are groping for—listeners equipped by Christian conviction, training, and experience to minister to them in very delicate, sometimes even rather public, circumstances. These are vulnerable, hurting fellow humans. They need what the church has to offer. But the Christian visitor has to know how to share in such a way that the other can receive his or her gift with integrity.

The hospital patient's relatives and friends often need help too. At times even nurses need to talk. Theirs is an increasingly demanding profession, both physically and emotionally. Individuals on the parish team of lay pastoral visitors, through the ministry of creative listening, can be a blessing to all of these. The value of this ministry extends far beyond the help it gives to individuals directly affected by it. Lay visitors from the parish can perform a very useful role of liaison between the institution and the praying congregation. In the opposite direction they can do a tremendous job of public relations for the church in the eyes of hospital officialdom, thus creating more opportunity for ministry. Few Christians seem aware of the possibilities for local missionary outreach through creative listening to individuals at home, in the community, and in hospital. People, especially those in hospital, are keenly aware of their own needs. Lay pastoral visitors who know how to deport themselves wisely and appropriately as trained listeners are amazed at the receptivity they find in such persons. This in itself is an incentive and reward for the time and effort they put into training for and practicing their calling.

This book grew out of a very practical need. I've been training lay pastoral visitors during the past five years, and a lay team now works with me in the hospital. We have met regularly over the years for prayer, discussion, and instruction according to the members' current experiences and requirements. Their request for a more structured input led to my designing a lecture series, dealing with practical situations that these volunteers discovered in their visiting. Later an invitation came from Dr Stackhouse, principal of Wycliffe College in the University of Toronto, to deliver these lectures in the

Wycliffe Lay School of Theology. I gave them the title, "Introduction to Lay Pastoral Visitation." When I started giving the Wycliffe lectures, I looked around for resource material, something to recommend to the students as a handbook, a sort of visitors' guide. I fully realize that no book or course of lectures can change a person into a good visitor. I simply wanted something that would give enquirers an idea of what hospital visiting is like, what some of the things are that an aspiring visitor should think about before plunging into this ministry, plus some practical instruction for the neophyte visitor. In my search I found plenty of literature written specifically for professional ministers – textbooks on counseling and pastoralia. I realize, of course, that many lay persons can benefit from such works, even though they are written for the "professionals." But I wanted something produced specifically for the non-professional. This is it.

The purpose of this book will be amply fulfilled if pastors and chaplains find it useful in forming and training lay pastoral visiting teams, if individual visitors gain inspiration and practical guidance, if lay teams use it for study and discussion. I hope that pastors themselves, especially those just out of seminary or Bible college, will appreciate its practical, evangelical approach. To this day there remains a dearth of practical pastoral training for many seminarians. Theological excellence, liturgical artistry, and evangelistic techniques are emphasized in many institutions that prepare persons for ordination. The provision for training people how to minister to other people is far from universal.

The ideas in the book come from a variety of sources – from my general reading, from pastors and counselors I've met and observed, from my own experience as a pastor, teacher, and chaplain. My students and trainees have taught me a great deal, and I acknowledge my debt to them. The principles of team formation and team learning I acquired from the Indiana Plan for Adult Education in the Church, during doctoral studies at Indiana University.

Before closing this preface, I would like to acknowledge my debt to my daughter Margaret and her husband Jamie Jordan, who spurred me to begin writing by presenting me, one Christmas, with a book full of blank pages. Inside the cover they had written, "To Donald Naylor Peel. This book is lovingly given for Christmas 1977 in anticipation of the great book you are going to write soon. Meg and Jamie." I thank Alice, my wife, from the bottom of my heart for her love and patience, and my daughter Mary for typing the manuscript. Finally, I salute North York General Hospital in whose warm atmosphere and stimulating environment the ideas for this book took shape. In this book the visitor is always a man and the patient is always a woman. I've kept it this way with the idea that maintaining consistency in these roles would make for easier reading.

1

Why Visit?

Why visit the sick? To a Christian the answer may seem obvious, but let's explore the matter. It will add to our sense of purpose and self-confidence to be able to state clearly why this ministry is so important. There are various reasons why Christians should visit the sick, and why some Christians have a special calling to this particular area of service instead of to some other ministry.

The first reason is very simple. *We have our Lord's express desire that we visit our sick.* "I was sick and ye visited me," he said. "Inasmuch as ye have done it unto the least of these my brethren ye have done it unto me" (Matt. 25:36,40). A word of caution is necessary here, because I have known Christians to interpret these words in such a way that they become distressed at their inability to visit sick persons. They fear that by failing to measure up, they will lose God's grace and his reward — an all too common neurotic dread, and a practical denial of the fact that salvation is by grace through faith, "not of works lest any man should boast" (Eph. 2:8–9). Their anxiety may take another form, namely, that their faith in Christ is inadequate. Feeling nervous, apprehensive, or even reluctant about calling on the sick, they go on comparing themselves to the outgoing, sparkling personalities whom they hear in rallies or see on TV. When they look at themselves, they appear in contrast to be very backward Christians.

But Jesus does not demand that we qualify for his love or that we measure up to the expectations others may have of us. He wants us to know that he does indeed love us. He died for us. He asks that we respond to his love with our own love for him, and in that love do the best we can. As we do this, we'll grow in ability both to love him and to express love to others. He may lead us on to great achievements. Or our exploits may be quiet, private, and quite low-key. Whatever he enables us to do and to achieve, we are his workers, and he gladly accepts what we offer (Eph. 2:10). Sick-visiting is not a means of qualifying to be a Class A Christian, or a way of earning God's favour. Even Jesus did not visit all the sick of his day, nor all the prisoners. He actually avoided them at times. He often tried to get away from the demanding crowds to find in prayer the fulfillment of his own needs. So just be your own kind of expression of God's love wherever you are. Work in the type of ministry for which he has fitted you. It may not be in the specialty of hospital work. You and his people can discern the work for which he is gifting you.

Do not visit the sick to allay your own anxiety. A visit made in this frame of mind will not comfort the patient. She'll sense that it is your guilt and not her need that motivates your visit. She may even end up ministering to you! Of course there's nothing wrong with this, and we thank God for such patients. But what of the patients that cannot minister to you — the ones who desperately need ministry from you, but whose needs you can't meet because you're inwardly still working on your own? Your encounter with a patient like that could end up doing more harm than good. If you feel this sort of guilty compulsion, do not begin visiting the sick until you have worked through your problem with some competent Christian counselor. Until such time visit only people whom you know well. And go with no other motive than to show that in Christ's love you care enough to call on them. No ulterior motive. No hidden agenda. No other goal.

When I think of the Inasmuch. . . principle, this first reason for visiting the sick, I think almost automatically of Mother Teresa of Calcutta. When I lived in India I met one of the groups that belongs to her order. They love people, even the most revoltingly sick and destitute. These women go about the streets of Calcutta to help dying people. They pick them up, put them on rickshaws, and take them to their own place. There they wash them, lay them on clean sheets, and tenderly feed and care for them until they die, serving them as though they were serving Christ himself. There on the filthy street or on the clean floor of their hospice, these nuns see not mere bedraggled, wrecked, and useless lives, but Christ, their Lord. Ignatius Loyola's prayer expresses it well: "To labor and not to seek for any reward, save that of knowing that we do thy will."

I have known Christians who would criticize Mother Teresa's mission. They'd say her ministry to the sick is inadequate because she does not preach the gospel with a view to converting the sick. The truth of the matter is, however, that Christ is preached because of her compassionate service. And he is preached not only by deeds but also in words! People constantly question her motives and the meaning of her unique ministry. She explains then about Christ: who he is, what he did, what he taught, how he died for our sins and rose, how he lives, and what he means to her. She tells not only individuals but vast audiences in halls, in front of TV screens, and people who read books about her. Thus Christ is made known, most definitely, as a result of her ministry. But the immediate goal of her ministry is not to preach but to love and serve the needy.

A second reason for visiting the sick is that we are members of Christ's body. When a Christian visits a sick person, there is a real sense in which Christ himself has visited that person. When you walk into the sickroom, Christ walks in. There is no presumption in such a statement. Christ is there in the person of yourself, for you are a member of him, an extension of his Person. This fact is especially meaningful when the patient also is a Christian and recognizes in you another part of the body of Christ to which she belongs. She can see in you, if she has eyes to see, and can feel through your visit, if she indeed believes the scriptures, not merely the practical outworking of a biblical doctrine but the real presence of Jesus.

Incidentally, this doctrinal and experiential truth of the body of Christ is a very good reason for not expecting the ordained ministers of the church to do all the parish sick-visiting. Clergy these days are hard pressed to fulfil the manifold functions that people expect of them: ministry to the sick, pastoral care of all church members, teaching, administration, evangelism, public relations, counselling, and preaching — to mention only a few. An impossible task! The church pastor cannot do it all alone. I believe he shouldn't even try! It is abundantly clear from scripture that the Holy Spirit gives ministerial gifts not just to clergy but to all Christians, as he wills. (Rom. 12, 1 Cor. 12, Ephesians 4, and 1 Peter 4 list some of these gifts.) It's up to the whole Christian body to discern what ministerial gifts God is giving to whom, and to make it possible for people to exercise their gifts.

Some lay people undoubtedly are gifted with the basic temperament, the motivation, and the spititual gifts for a specialized ministry in what could be called lay chaplaincy. It is important for such people to realize that being thus endowed does not eliminate for them the urgency to take training to enhance their natural and spiritual gifts. Rather it increases the obligation to develop the divine "investment" toward the achievement of excellence. The church ought to be alert to discern those who seem gifted for such a ministry and to urge them to take training for the better implementation of their gift.

When I speak about gifts and temperaments that can be enhanced by training and the acquisition of relational skills, I may seem to contradict what the experts in management education are saying. They argue that there is no such thing as a "born leader," that there are no inherent qualities in leaders, that successful training can bring about personal change and make a person into a leader. However, we're not dealing with that kind of leadership. We're speaking of love and caring — motivational qualities, relational attitudes, ministerial leadership. A patient can sense, sooner or later, when a visitor is using learned techniques without real warmth, and when he is showing real love through carefully learned techniques. There's a difference! The distinction may seem fine, but I'm sure it's there. No technical finesse can substitute for the love of Christ. That love cannot be "switched on" when needed. I'm afraid some leaders are not the same people at home as they are in the office or plant. Their leadership skills are learned behaviors, tacked on to their personalities for the accomplishment of specific business or industrial goals. But the mature Christian minister, like Jesus, is ideally always the same: a "together" person whose real self and professional self are not divided, but one whole self. This is the reality at the basis of one-to-one ministry. The innate qualities count very much indeed, and the helping skills serve as effective vehicles. A good definition of Christian leadership might be: the ministry of encouraging and facilitating the exercise and development by God's people of the ministries to which God is calling them and for which he is gifting and equipping them.

A third reason to visit the sick is that the patient has very human needs: his need for friendship, for being loved, for meaning, for sense of worth, for understanding. We visit the sick in the name of Christ chiefly for their benefit, not ours, but it would be unrealistic to deny that *some of the visitor's needs are met* in the process. Would it be imprudent to suggest that *this be considered a fourth reason* for visiting the sick? Let not what has been disaffirmed above (about visiting to relieve one's own anxieties) blind us to the truth that showing love and caring does something for the visitor too, meeting his or her need to love, to have a sense of worth and meaning, to grow as a person.

Another by-product of ministering to patients is that *we can learn from the experiences we undergo* to be more sensitive to people's needs, more discerning, more understanding, more skilful in ministering to everyone. The learnings are transferable to all helping relationships: at home, in parish work, in Sunday school, with neighbors. The more we minister to the sick, the better we become at ministering in general. With this in mind many clergy take training in hospitals and prisons, some with a view to becoming chaplains, others with the idea of gaining, from this concentrated ministry to people in crisis, experience to help them in their whole ministry and in all their relationships. In this high ministry lay people participate with the professionals in the healing ministry of Christ. There are inestimable benefits for both patient and visitor. Our chief concern is to be willing and able vehicles for the operation of the grace of Christ and the help of persons in need.

The Lay Pastoral Visiting Team

One of the most effective ways to visit in hospital is to develop a lay pastoral visiting team. The team meets once every two or three weeks during a training period. A great deal of sharing goes on in these meetings, so that almost everyone is stimulated by the encouragement he or she receives and contributes. As chaplain and team leader, I find myself sharing out of my own experience, referring the team to pastoral textbooks or biblical examples, challenging the group to use imagination in a team approach to problem solving. Learning inevitably takes place because these visitors are so eager, so very much involved in their pastoral situations. They are highly motivated to grow in new insights, new attitudes, and improved skills.

A careful screening process takes place before any person joins the team. Individual motivation or individual sense of calling to this ministry is important, but it must be confirmed. Persons aspiring to membership on the team agree to have their suitability for hospital ministry assessed by their own ministers and by myself. The calling is "not of private interpretation." Each candidate is asked to take an introductory course on lay pastoral visiting, or some equivalent course.[1]

Having been accepted for the team, new members are required to make certain commitments: to visit in the hospital under my supervision, to come regularly to team meetings, and to agree, should any one of us begin to feel that a particular visitor's ministry and vocation may not be in hospital ministry but perhaps in some other sphere of service, to "speak the truth in love" about it and discuss steps toward his discovering a ministry elsewhere. Then begins a period of internship or "advanced" training under supervision. Such supervised ministry is a common element in all effective training. An interweaving of content and practical experience, with repeated opportunities for joint reflection, are basic to this process. Such internship is practiced not only in hospitals, but in churches too.[2]

The purpose of courses and team meetings is only partly concerned with adding a new set of principles, ideas, doctrines, and methods to the visitor's existing store of intellectual information. The goal is for team members, by means of reflection on and discussion about actual experiences of visiting, to become more aware of their own strengths and weaknesses, to learn from their own and others' mistakes, to increase in the understanding and perception of patients' needs, to learn practical ways of improving their visiting skills, to be forewarned and forearmed to avoid possible blunders, to familiarize themselves with hospital settings and modes of operation, to learn how they can show in appropriate ways that God cares and that they care too, to discover their pastoral gifts and to develop them, to become aware of their own feelings toward the sick and the dying and by God's grace to deal with those feelings constructively, and finally, to learn how to help patients in ways that the patients themselves are able to receive that help.

An overwhelming expectation? Yes, if you feel you have to become perfect within the first twenty years of pastoral visiting. But not if you go at it with the attitude that you want to grow a little week by week, along with your team-mates. The goal is stated not in a preconceived set of absolute standards, but rather in areas of desired growth and improvement. It's a process of helping each other to "grow up in every way into Christ" as Saint Paul stated in Ephesians 4:15. His words could very well be adopted as a theme for the whole movement of team ministry.

2

Focus On The Patient

This book is about the ministry of listening. We haven't got into the specifics of it up to this point because it helps to have an idea beforehand of what people are like — not in order to cast them all in the same mold but to stimulate our awareness and adjust our attitudes toward their real needs so that we approach them in an appropriate frame of mind. Who is this person who watches with boredom or delight our approach to her bedside? What goes on in her mind? Is that the wary expression of a prisoner or the pained look of an unwilling martyr? If only we could see the patient as God sees her. We need to know her in her many human aspects — spiritually, denominationally, socially, culturally, psychologically, developmentally — one person in all her rich complexity.

We must avoid viewing people with doctrinal blinkers or culturally tinted lenses, which can only result in our ministering out of a very restricted apprehension of who they really are and what they really need. Visitors who approach their vocation with any kind of restricted or inadequate understanding of people can fail to minister to God's ailing creature, and instead try to "work on" a client who is made in their own narrow image and in the likeness of their own unexamined prejudice. Through ignorance or stubbornness they see people through lenses that distort or blinkers that hide half the picture. Have you looked at yourself to see whether you are wearing any? They can keep you from really meeting the patient. Here is a brief list.[3]

1 First are the "what-is-God-trying-to-say-to-you-through-this" blinkers. If this is the only theme on the visitor's mind, it will keep him from hearing what the patient is crying out for.

2 The "jolly entertainer's" blinkers are worn by visitors who avoid being moved by the reality of sickness. They spend their time indiscriminately trying to cheer up everyone they visit.

3 The visitor who wears the gray lenses of Job's comforters continually argues, "You must have sinned. That is why you are ill. Measure up, and God will reward you with health."

4 One kind of blinker causes the visitor to regard lack of healing as proof that the person is weak in faith.

5 There are rose-colored lenses that transform the evil of suffering into something wonderful, a gift for which we must thank God because he has inflicted it for a good purpose. Sometimes the prayer of thanksgiving is recommended as a sort of gimmick which we hope will change or remove the suffering.

6 Some people wear blinkers that block out reality. Sickness to them is not real.

7 Then there is the visitor who wears "laying-on-of-hands" blinkers. Laying on of hands is this person's inflexible agenda in the sickroom.

8 Some visitors wear "express-your-anger" blinkers, regarding physical illness as a sign of repressed hostility. They spend all their time trying to get people to express anger.

9 Psychological blinkers cause visitors to interpret a patient's condition according to their favourite theory.

10 Blinkers made of *Four Spiritual Laws* and other such pamphlets prevent the visitor from seeing the patient because of his own zealous enthusiasm.

Let me hasten to add that the above or any other prefabricated blinkers or lenses are made of fragments of the whole truth. I assure you that I do believe in miracles. Assuredly, too, right thinking and good psychology help toward wholeness. Accepting Christ as Saviour is supremely important, and does result in amazing and demonstrable differences in people's lives. To praise God is healthy. Laying on of hands is scriptural. We must hold to these truths. We also must not allow any one of them or any other truths to be used as doctrinaire prejudgments that restrict our ability to discern in genuine warm encounter who the patient, is and what her immediate needs are. If we were not forewarned to put off these blinkers in order to serve the patient we might tend to see her more as a splendid target for our special theories and techniques, and fail really to help her.

Who is the Patient?

Let's look at the patient in a theological context. This will put her into perspective for us, and we'll come closer to seeing her as God does. Let us also make ourselves aware of some of the common experiences and feelings that hospital patients have, so that we'll spot them the instant they appear. We must take careful note that no two patients are exactly alike. Every person we visit is unique: unique in origins, in genetic make-up, in development, in experience, in family background, education, and personality; unique in attitudes, feelings, and emotions; with different gifts, talents, lifestyles, jobs, interests, resources, connections, skills, and needs. To generalize is impossible, to stereotype insulting and dangerous. With that caveat let us proceed.

The Bible tells us that *every human being is created in the image of God.* Because of this we can be sure that every person we visit is infinitely valuable, intrinsically so because of the value with which the Creator invests him or her. Therefore we, the Creator's messengers, must regard each one as special, worthy of our respect and care because loved by God and infinitely precious to him. Also, as Mother Teresa's example constantly reminds us, there is a very real sense in which each patient is Christ to us, Christ, that is, in need of our ministry and service. The patients you and I have occasion to visit are not always derelict. Nevertheless the same principle of ministry applies: "Ye visited me."

Some of the patients you will visit are Christian and therefore, as we have noted, *fellow members of the body of Christ.* This doctrine, deeply believed, can affect our entire attitude toward the brother or sister we're visiting. The Christian patient is a member of you, "for we are members one of another" (Eph. 4:25). This means that in ministering to her you minister to yourself. In another context (Eph. 5:29) Saint Paul declared that no man in his right mind ever hates his own flesh but sees to its health and welfare as lovingly as the Lord watches over the church. Knowing this can help us to relate fittingly to a fellow believer. The Christian patient's suffering is yours too, as also is her recovery and rejoicing (1 Cor. 12:25-26). Being parts of the one body, each has a vested interest in the wellbeing of the other.

One of your Christian patient's needs is to be able to feel these truths. Even though the patient were incapable intellectually of grasping the doctrine of the Body, she can be helped to feel that she is a member of Christ. Brainpower is not the final test of belonging to the Lord. Great numbers of Christians experience the feeling of body membership long before being able to verbalize or conceptualize the fact of it. The same can be said of the children of Christians. The experience is the Holy Spirit's gift to the simplest believer. There is a real sense, therefore, in which your just being there from the church is an unspoken proclamation to the patient of these marvellous truths. Your visit can even be a first step toward awakening her awareness of the body to which she as a believer belongs.

The patient is still growing, as we hope you are too. Most of us still have a long way to go to be what God created us to become. You can afford to be patient with her, while "speaking the truth in love." To be more specific about this, your Christian friend on the sickbed may have some faulty attitudes and habits. Her mental hygiene may leave all kinds of room for improvement. She may be in spiritual doldrums. Her behaviour may upset you. You may even think to yourself, as you leave the hospital, such things as, "Why in heaven's name can't she change that critical, complaining attitude of hers? Everybody's trying to help her, but she just won't make use of anybody's help. Doesn't she know God loves her, for goodness' sake? What a whiner!"

Yes, it can be very irritating. More so because a Christian isn't "supposed" to have those sorts of feelings and reactions. So it helps to realize that though your patient may be far from mature, she probably hasn't "arrived" yet. But then, neither have you. You're both imperfect.

The Patient's Needs

There are *some universal human needs* which we can safely assume without prejudicing our attitude toward the individual patient. Various writers, psychologists, and psychiatrists have brought these to the attention of the reading public. They are needs which any student of the Bible and of human nature will immediately recognize and acknowledge.

First of all is the need to be loved. [4]Reuel Howe in *Man's Need and God's Action* relates what is now fairly common knowledge: that babies can survive a lot of hardships and stresses, but without love they die. Life loses its value without love. All our patients need to feel loved. Some Christians talk as if loving others were a means to some end, a step toward conversion or some other hoped-for change. Not so. Christian love is itself the goal. Love is, as Henry Drummond wrote in the last century, "the greatest thing in the world." God is love.

Secondly, we need to be able to express love. The Bible teaches neighbor. People who do are healthy from the core of their being. We all need to be able to give love as well as to receive it.
We all need to be able to love as well as to give love.

Thirdly, we need a sense of worth, a feeling that we're valuable, needed, good to have around, able to make a worthwhile contribution to other peoples' lives and to God's world.

Fourthly, we need a sense of meaning, to know that our lives and the things that happen to us (such as illness) make some kind of sense – even if only to God. Dr Victor Frankl found that prisoners of World War II who had some reason to live, a sense of purpose in life, could survive almost anything.[5] A person will even prefer suffering to pleasure if that is the only way his or her life can have meaning. On the other hand, any prisoner who lost faith in his future just gave up and usually died. Meaning is not simply an attitude that a person creates for himself. It is the acceptance of what life expects of him. In Christian language that is the acceptance of God's purpose for creation and for each one of us.

We should add that *fifthly, all people need forgiveness,* to be forgiven and to forgive others. We need to be reconciled to God, to enjoy loving and being loved by him, and also to be reconciled to one another, rescued from the sense of alienation which besets human kind. By being aware of these universal human needs within ourselves, we will be able to recognize the same needs when expressed by the ones to whom we minister. Besides these universal human needs, you may expect to discover your patient experiencing one or another of the *immediate needs* described as follows.

Your patient may do a lot of thinking, or brooding, while confined to bed. She's probably wondering what earthly use she is to anyone. She may fear that she'll never again be able to do the things she used to do. Much of her thinking depends on how serious her illness is. She could be feeling very guilty about all the jobs that are being left undone because of her absence from home or business. She may be blaming herself for not taking the precautions that she imagines might have kept her from getting sick and hospitalized. She may be thinking about life, its values, about her need of God.

Shut-ins, especially hospital patients, *are separated from many aspects of normal living.* They feel cut off from their families, their churches, communities, and neighborhoods. Hospital buildings at times seem like prisons. They enclose people, restrict them, sever them from "life out there." More than one patient in delerium, and others quite alert to reality, have expressed to me *feelings of imprisonment.* Freedom is gone. One's whole life is being run by others.

Some of these things you may have experienced yourself, if you've ever been in hospital. You know, for example, how *time can hang very heavily*. The first week seems an eternity. It is very easy for a patient to become bored, restless, impatient, despondent. It is possible to reach a stage after several weeks or months when one loses track of time. All days are alike, and a week can go by leaving very little memory of it. In a way this is a blessing. On the other hand memory can fade too much. One can begin to feel stupid from the lack of activity and stimulation. Bare rooms add to the sterility of sensation. A person who knows how to minister to a patient suffering tedium can be a real bright spot in her day, even if the visit lasts only five minutes.

A certain amount of *regression* is not unusual for patients in hospital. They need to be looked after. They have to do what the doctor says, to obey the nurse, to take their medicine when they're told, to depend on others for just about everything, even for permission and assistance to go to the bathroom. Regression means lapsing into a habit of dependency. It means becoming less mature, less responsible, more childish. Doctor becomes "Big Daddy." He can hurt your feelings by paying you less attention than you crave or by talking crossly to you. He can make you feel rebellious, peevish, or simperingly goody-goody. A patient can be overindulged in childish regression to the extent of hampering recuperation. She should really become an adult partner in the healing team, co-operating fully with the doctor and staff.

Often the patient must even play a genuine *co-ordinating* role, functioning as an important communications link among her various therapists. An alert and responsible patient can help things a very great deal indeed. Many a nurse's error or omission in charting orders has been easily and simply rectified because a patient spoke up and declared, "But the doctor said. . ." What a patient often needs is not sympathy but stimulation, and at times challenge, to take responsibility for an important and vital part in her own healing. In other words, the patient needs to *co-operate with the natural healing and recuperative forces that God has built into her body*. The doctor himself is doing that very thing. The entire healing team needs to be part of this action—including the pastoral visitor.

It is common knowledge that a patient can interfere with and even block healing through negative attitudes and thoughts, such as fear, resentment, revenge, and plain "giving up." The will to live and the will to be healed are tremendously important factors in successful medicine. The pastoral visitor can encourage a patient to co-operate with the healing powers that God has placed within her. There are healing powers for the mind and the emotions as well. We must be aware of these. They are "on our side" against disease and for well-being.

The patient needs *faith, courage,* and *hope.* These are attitudes that your visit can inspire, usually without even mentioning the words. When a doctor refers some patient to the chaplain, often he's saying that the patient needs assistance to overcome discouragement and the temptation to give up. He knows that the patient won't improve if she does not will to. The visit of a Christian friend can help a patient decide to come out of a spiritual and mental nosedive, and to reach upward again. Many patients who can see their illness in perspective need no special help. Others desperately need the support and prayers of friends to maintain a sense of purpose in their lives.

The patient may be asking, "*Why has God done this to me?*" What sense does it all make? There may be many things she just cannot understand. It's hard for a patient to be philosophical when every nerve is screeching and nothing takes the pain away. Intense pain dissolves every other sensation into itself and, devil-like, demands unconditional capitulation. A patient in such condition is not ready for sermons. But a visitor who understands, even silently, can be a prayerful comfort. Jesus suffered wracking pain not only in his body but in his soul and spirit. His agony and subsequent victory can somehow help us in ours. Even in the "smaller" pains—the griefs and stresses of life, the agonies of operations and long stays in hospital—our having this sense of meaning, a sense especially of ultimate and eternal meaning in God, helps.[6]

As Cabot and Dicks point out in *The Art of Ministering to the Sick,* patients need *beauty.* It's good for everyone. How uplifting it is to experience a beautiful scene or garden, to enjoy the hospitality of charming people, to hear lovely music. So when you go to visit, make yourself as neat, clean, and presentable as you possibly can. Even if you happen not to be a devastatingly handsome or gorgeous person, do the best you can with what you've got so that you're pleasant to behold. The expression on your face when you enter the room is important. Let it be serene, not anxious, fearful, or dour. The beauty of a face is not in the features so much as in the heart and mind, and the beauty shines out.

The surroundings in the patient's room can bring the gift of beauty. Flowers (not too many), pictures, cards, restful happy colors—all these can help her mood, and contribute to a healing atmosphere. Have you ever walked into a hospital room, or any room for that matter, even in a home, and felt that things are not right? The patient's room should not give her messages of tension and depression. But it will if there is nothing to brighten it up. Bare cells are great for monks and for people whose purpose is to withdraw from the world; but they're no good for patients. They need beauty around them.

Patients need beauty in their thoughts and minds too. They need to read beauty and to think of it, to hear beauty as well as to see it. They should even wear beauty if at all possible—the hospital hairdresser can vouch for the value of that! And think of your conversation. There are more beautiful things to impress on the patient's mind than your own problems, the gory details of your last operation, or the dying symptoms of your deceased next-door neighbor.

Cabot and Dicks say that *quietness* is part of this beauty. Not the "shush-shush" tip-toe behavior, which can have the opposite effect of annoying the patient and even making her feel falsely guilty of being touchy, sensitive, and fragile. Healing quietness is more like the "peace of God that passeth all understanding." It is restfulness, a quietness that nourishes the soul. This quality may go with you into the room, or may be generated during your encounter. It's a spiritual quality, a kind of gracious acceptance by you of the patient. It's a thankful receptiveness in her to what God has to give. Confidence and trust between visitor and patient are two of its ingredients.

After the patient goes home her needs continue and new ones are added, especially these days when hospital stays are shorter and doctors think in terms of letting the patient finish her recuperation at home. Female patients probably are faced with the greatest difficulties in this regard. There are the difficulties of adjusting to the home situation, not having people to look after beds and laundry, pills and meals and dishes; having to see not only to one's own needs, but shouldering responsibility for children and husband as well. We'd do a great service to recuperating patients if in our churches and neighborhoods we organized parish visitors to give support, encouragement, and practical help to people newly arrived home from hospital.

3

The Visitor

For you to derive maximum benefit from this chapter, I suggest you read it once through now, then go on to study the rest of the book. When you've finished reading and have in your mind a picture of lay pastoral visiting, then come back to this point and consider again the qualities that help a person be a good visitor.

Who Is The Visitor?

Like the patient, the visitor is a child of God, loved and highly valued. Because he's a member of Christ's body, he and Christian patients are members of one another. I've described how this fact helps the visitor's presence say to the patient that God cares, that Jesus is with him or her. When we have this mental orientation, it makes a great difference in our attitudes and our effectiveness as visitors. In the previous chapter I also mentioned some universal human needs such as love, forgiveness, meaning, sense of worth. The visitor has as much need of these as do his patients.

The Visitor's Needs

Now I'd like to move on to some of the personal qualities, attitudes, and learned skills that make a good visitor—qualities and attitudes to look for when you're screening people for the team or thinking of specializing yourself, skills that will take some effort to learn and apply, but when acquired, will enable you by God's grace to excel in this calling.[7]

One attitude is *commitment to regular visiting*. Being a pastoral visitor is not a ministry that you do in your idle moments, when you happen to feel like it. Though it is a volunteer ministry, it is nevertheless a responsible one. Visitors who cannot be depended on to be faithful in their duties are very hard to work with and of little help to the patients. Quite often you won't be in the mood to visit, so what do you do? Trust God and go ahead. Do it because you're committed to it. You'll be surprised how God can bless you in the process. Sacrificially ministering to others can pull you out of the doldrums. John Wesley knew that by experience. He wrote in his journal how preaching the word to sinners would revitalize his flagging strength and cure his ailments. A member of the visiting team must be committed to his ministry just as the congregation's pastor is expected to be to his. Both are ministries of the body of Christ. Both involve the obedient exercise of the Spirit's gifts in answer to his call.

Self acceptance is a necessary quality for a pastoral visitor. The opposite of this is "putting yourself down" or being unable to live with yourself. Self acceptance means accepting God's acceptance of you in Christ. It means seeing yourself with all your good points and your bad ones, recognizing that God loves you and can use you just the way you are. When thinking of self-acceptance, don't neglect your good points! Write them all down. Thank God for them! Try the following exercise sometime. Get a group of people together who are interested in serving others, and instruct them to write down all their good and bad points on two sides of a sheet of notepaper. Almost without fail they will find no trouble filling one half of the page with their bad points, but will have immense difficulty getting more than four or five good ones written on the opposite side of the page.

The visitor needs *an ability to evaluate his own strengths and weaknesses.* Take a good objective look at yourself. Ask your trusted friends or team members for a little help. You may be blessed with abundant patience, able to listen for hours on end. You may have plenty of physical energy. Or perhaps you can zero in on the problem that's bothering a person. You may be not only a talented problem-finder but an efficient problem-solver too. Whatever your strong points are, work to improve them and put them to good use. Step forward! Volunteer! "Work out your own salvation with fear and trembling, knowing that God is working in you both to will and to do of his good pleasure" (Phil. 2:12,13). That's not arrogance. It's humble and grateful realism.

Another important requirement for the visitor is an ability to *accept others the way they are,* for the same reasons that you accept yourself. "Accept one another as Christ has accepted you, for the Glory of God" (Rom. 15:7). We're on the Way together, and the going often gets hard. Let's welcome and help one another on our pilgrimage. The verse in Romans applies primarily to Christians, but we must visit the unbeliever too with the same love and acceptance that Christ himself gives.

The visitor will also need some *initiative.* He'll have to plan his own visits, make his own way, create openings for conversation, seek out resources and aids. He should not always have to work under the direction of somebody else or depend overly on the good-will and permission of staff who may not adequately understand his ministry. The visitor needs to be a self-starter and a self-propeller, able when necessary to work on his own. The visitor therefore needs the ability to *make contacts* and then to flow with the feelings of the other. In order to do this he'll have to communicate as an *active and creative listener*.

A pastoral visitor must have *good physical and emotional health*. If you're tired all the time, just dragging yourself around, it's hard to concentrate on the conversation. This requires attentive listening, trying to discover "where the patient is at," watching for clues to her feelings and needs, sensing what she's reaching for. You can't do any of this properly if you're continually worn out or in bad health. Illness is bound to interfere with the regularity of your visiting as well. This applies to the visitor's emotional health too. A stable, level-headed, steady type of person stands a better chance of becoming a good visitor than one who has emotional problems or neurotic hang-ups. The person who is in good mental health, who is aware of his own feelings and knows how to deal with them appropriately, is more likely to focus his attention entirely on the patient's needs and to minister to her.

It is necessary for a visitor to have *a deep respect for the patient's religious convictions*. He can do this only if he feels secure within himself and if his own faith is strong. From the vantage of his own assurance he can accept the other person as she is, accord her the right to her own beliefs, and relate to her as a peer. The visitor will find himself conversing with people of many Christian denominations and other faiths. In some hospitals the team members have the responsibility of visiting all patients on a certain unit. They may call on anyone in that unit who might benefit from their ministry. Or the nurse may make a referral: "I wish you'd visit Mrs Smith." Mrs Smith turns out to be, say, Jewish or Ukranian Orthodox, and you're Plymouth Brethren. How do you minister?

You need *to be able humbly and lovingly to share your faith* with the patient when the opportunity opens up. There is no need to scheme or to use guile. You don't go in with a predetermined agenda to wangle the conversation around to what you want to say. The focus is on her and her need, not on your agenda. You go in with full respect for the patient, just as she is, beliefs and all. And you minister to her immediate needs out of Christ's love within you. I have great confidence in the truth of Christianity, especially in its teaching about humanity's need for reconciliation with God in Christ. And I'm sure, in fact I know from experience, that those deep needs are going to be expressed sooner or later, if you're a good listener, at a point when your patient will be glad to hear you share your faith. People in hospital are very vulnerable. The patient is at the mercy of anyone bold enough to barge in and impose on her. One of the services she needs is protection from people she doesn't want to see, a safeguard from religious zealots who, seeing the patient as a captive audience, might pounce on her as a likely convert.

Some *facility in theological reflection on his own ministry* is important for the pastoral visitor. This means not only thinking about God, Man, Christ, and his work. It means trying to perceive how God was working in that last visit, what he was doing with the patient and with the visitor himself. Reflecting in this manner, as a group, will help the team members to understand their various individual encounters and to interpret each others' experiences. We don't need a degree in divinity to see God's action in the world. One can reflect on this at any time on the basis of one's current theological understanding. What will happen through reflection and discussion in the team, however, is that the members will be stimulated to read more, to listen and learn more, to equip themselves better for their ministry.

The visitor needs some practical knowledge and skill too. *A thorough orientation to the hospital itself* is necessary. Getting to know your way around the building is basic to feeling at home there and feeling at ease in your visiting. Find out where you can go and from where you must stay away. Know the fire drill. Learn the meanings of the various codes that come over the PA system. The more familiar you are with all these things, the more confident and at ease you'll feel on the job.

If you visit regularly in one hospital, *get to know the staff.* They are frantically busy at times, but they're human. When you're on good terms with them, all kinds of good things are possible. Much time is saved that could otherwise be spent going to wrong rooms or trying to find someone who isn't there any more. The staff will give you bits of advice too, perhaps even some understanding of procedures that can save you from bungles, misunderstandings, and hard feelings. One young helper of mine, feeling very much at home in the hospital, peeked one day into what he thought was an empty operating room only to be greeted with "Get the hell out of here.

Don't you know this is an operating room?" That makes for poor rapport! Know your limits. Be fully oriented.

A visitor should *know about the helping resources in the community and the hospital*. There are social workers in most hospitals to whom you can make referrals. If you know the worker, you can suggest he might be able to help a patient with a particular practical problem. There are psychologists on staff too. Community clergy of many denominations are available through the chaplain. The Public Health Department serves the needy of the municipality, including discharged patients and relatives of patients. Most communities provide family services and services to the aged. There are epileptic societies, leukemia societies, multiple sclerosis societies, and others. There is Alcoholics Anonymous. Books, pamphlets, and directories are available which list all community service agencies. You can obtain these just by asking around.[8] If you don't have access to the information yourself, it is good to know how to find it.

A pastoral visitor will need two other skills. The first is a *knowledge of the scriptures*. What I refer to here is neither theological virtuosity nor a flair for Christian apologetics. I mean familiarity with the various portions of the Bible that speak to specific longings of the heart and problems common to the human lot — passages that express yearning, perplexity, or comfort. The visitor's ministry will be enhanced greatly if he can recall, at a moment's notice, a scriptural thought that speaks to the patient's situation, gives her food for thought, or provides her with a promise to cling to. The beginner may feel that his store of scriptural knowledge is meager. No need to despair. It can be learned.

Finally, the visitor will need to *be able to pray aloud for people*. You'll be asked to do this sooner or later, even if you don't offer in response to a desire that you discern in a patient. I'm not urging you to acquire the "gift of the gab" with God. Soaring lyrics of mellifluous prose spiced with Bible verses and replete with the rich vocabulary of your particular stream of Christian tradition — this is not what I mean by the ability to pray out loud! The long-suffering patient may be impressed but will be little helped by verbal dexterity alone. What the patient needs is prayer that speaks to God simply and realistically on her behalf, bringing to our heavenly Father her situation, needs, feelings, and concerns, and asking humbly for grace.

Who, then, is the visitor, and what does he need? In summary, he's human and needs the things that all people need—love, a sense of meaning, and a feeling of worth. He needs acceptance and assurance of God's forgiveness and grace. He needs to acknowledge and deal with his own emotional needs. He needs to become familiar with scripture and conversant in prayer.

4

The Art Of
Creative Listening

Everyone loves a good listener. Dale Carnegie observed this and made a lot of money with his book *How To Win Friends and Influence People*. He advised his readers to practice the art of listening. People like to be listened to. Not only do they like it; they need it. Giving an understanding and attentive ear really helps them. It makes them your friends as well. But there is more to a listening ministry than just making friends. The title of Carnegie's book may imply a selfish motive. Undoubtedly one could adopt that attitude. However, one can also use the art of listening for purposes that grow out of caring, prompted by a concern to demonstrate the love of Christ and to help other people.

I was sitting in the cafeteria of the hospital one day, when the infection control nurse came and joined me for her coffee break. We exchanged pleasantries, and I began my usual gentle probing for conversational clues. "How's the work going?" "I enjoyed your lecture the other day." But it was not long before I realized that she had been listening to clues in *my* remarks. By showing an interest in me, my work, my goals and interest, she had me talking and thoroughly enjoying the experience of being listened to. In a warm and genuine way she related to me as a person and understood my need. It was not dramatic or desperate. I was just tired and frazzled, but she cared, and made it easy for me to express my feelings. It was a most refeshing coffee break.

Charles Truax and Robert Carkhuff, in their research report *Toward Effective Counseling and Psychotherapy*, show that successful therapists, no matter what their school of thought, display in their behavior toward clients three important qualities: nondefensive genuineness, nonpossessive warmth, and accurate empathy. You too can bring these qualities to the patients you visit. Any dialogue worthy of the name demands that one of the participants listen carefully. Most of your visits will give you the opportunity to practice creative listening, no matter how short, long, or deep your conversation may be.

Depending on the circumstances of the person you visit, a dialogue can take various directions. One might conceivably attach labels to the different parts, or even the whole, of a conversation: ventilating, problem-solving, spiritual search, lighthearted exchange. Whatever the topic, a creative listener can pick up signals from the patient about her needs. That's what the infection-control nurse friend did for me. The main gist of your conversation with someone in hospital may be the reminiscences of two old friends. Your chronic patient may be eager for news of home, friends, school, the community. Your time on the first visit may be spent mostly in getting to know each other. Or the patient may openly reveal her need for help of some kind, perhaps even for "spiritual" advice.

In the midst of all this, how do you pick up cues and what do you do with them? Is the purpose of creative listening only to make the patient feel good, or are there other goals?

What Is Creative Listening?

In defining creative listening I would like to distinguish, first of all, between passive and active listening. Active listening is more creative, although passive listening too can produce extremely beneficial results, depending on the circumstances and the persons involved.

In passive listening the other person talks and you listen. You may say, "Aha, yes, aha, mmm, yes, ahum, aha. . ." that is, you make sounds to indicate to the other person that she has your attention. You may even repeat snatches of what she says, so that she is encouraged to continue.

You have to be careful, though, not to wander off into daydreams while the speaker rattles on. If you do, you might find yourself saying "aha" where it's far from appropriate. Even passive listening is work. You have to stay alert.

In what circumstances can passive listening be creative? I'll mention only a few. Some elderly people who are lonely seem to obtain a sense of worth out of reminiscing about earlier exploits and loves and interests. Another patient may need to pour out his feelings, perhaps in a sort of confession or catharsis. Reliving a bereavement or a loss by telling all about it can be very helpful. I recall vividly how much I was helped when a clergyman friend of mine listened with great patience while I was mourning my father's death.

The listener using this approach has very little control over the content of the conversation. The patient or client chooses what she will tell. I know there are some people who talk so much and so fast that you can't get a word in edgewise, even if you want to. I have my doubts about the benefits of listening endlessly to them. They're compulsive talkers, and they need another kind of ministry. A really creative listener recognizes when the other truly needs someone who will "listen to her story" for the sake of her mental and spiritual health. It takes patience. It takes alertness. But if you're being a doormat, there's something wrong.

Active listening, on the other hand, is work of a different kind. It requires more skill. But you can begin this kind of ministry with whatever ability you have at the moment and learn to improve your skill as you go along. A passive listener may partway through a conversation switch his technique to active listening. In active listening the visitor indicates by his replies that he's caught the patient's mood, her feeling, her concern. He thus provides an opportunity for the speaker to express more feeling if she wishes, or to clarify or expand on what she's already said.

The active listener tries to be especially aware of feelings, but responds to them without ignoring the actual content of the conversation. He therefore needs to be doubly alert. He picks up clues about worries, fears, anger, resentment, joys, convictions, depression, appreciations, hope, aspirations — all the varied colors and motions of the patient's personality and need. The purpose is not, however, to precipitate an emotional binge. What the active listener really does is to make it easy for the patient to be herself, openly to talk about her real feelings and, in many instances, honestly to face her situation. To put it another way, the purpose of active listening is to enable a person to make use of you, the listener, to help her deal with her own needs and grow as a person. The idea then is not for you to solve her problem, or even to give advice. You act somewhat like a talking mirror, reflecting back to her what you hear, see, or sense. To this you may add the occasional brief comment. Through this exchange the patient very often will come to her own conclusions or find her own solutions.[9]

When a patient has a good listener, she is able to make her own adjustments and respond to the healing grace of God. As Saint Paul suggests, she learns to work out her salvation in her own way, perhaps through a different approach to life or through a decision to take a new step in her earthly pilgrimage (Phil. 2:13–13). When functioning as an active listener, you do not let the client control the conversation. You and she together determine its direction and subject matter. But you take the lead. This does not mean that you do most of the talking either. Usually you'll say very little. But what you do say has the effect of steering the conversation into fruitful channels, provided the client willingly responds — and she does if the rapport is good. In a two-way dialogue there is no manipulation. You react to the feelings she shows and the things she says in such a way that she senses your interest. This prompts her to bring matters into the open where she can deal with them. The active listener tries to sense where the patient really wants to go, and assists her in that pilgrimage.

To some readers this ministry may seem much easier than they had previously thought. The burden of having to know all the answers is removed, and the visitor does not have to feel responsible for solving the patient's problems. Others may consider the listening ministry too technical, and cringe at the enormity of the challenge to help someone change in faith, resolution, hope — in whatever area of life growth is needed. To the first I say that this ministry is not by any means smooth sailing. It's a delicate, and sensitive, and often draining task. I once heard Dr Elisabeth Kubler-Ross declare that talking with dying people is such a strain that even a professional could not be expected to do it for more than three or four hours a day. The same emotional drain is felt by people who talk constantly with the sick. This ministry is not easy. It's work — a labour of love.

To those in the other category I say: please realize that perfection is impossible, if for no other reason than there are no solid criteria for evaluating success. As long as you do no actual harm to the patient (Florence Nightingale's first dictum for nurses), then simply by being warm, honest, and alert to the cues your patient gives, you are already engaged on an elementary level in the basics of active listening. The work of change is not something you can set out resolutely to achieve or to impose on anyone. You do not coerce patients into changing. The doctor treats, but it is the patient who gets well, through the natural forces of recuperation within her. Likewise you treat, by listening and trusting in God's power, but God Himself brings about healing.

It is important at this point to take note of one thing that creative listening is not. It should not incite the patient to "sound off" or "get things off her chest" in the sense of expressing or acting out her anger. Fashionable though this approach may be in some schools of therapy, forcefully expressing anger and resentment often produces no other effect than to develop an ingrained habit of wallowing in fury, of acting out infantile and unproductive emotions.

Don't misunderstand. Inner anger does have to be recognized, acknowledged, and expressed in appropriate ways. Jesus was often angry, as the gospels, especially Mark, record. We all need to learn how to deal creatively with our surges of strong feeling, particularly when they arise out of indignation or hurt. It is hardly the place of the lay pastoral visitor, however, to try educating patients about things that are the province of the trained counselor or therapist. A lay person might, with experience, recognize the patient's need for psycho-therapy or re-education and suggest that she talk with her minister or doctor about referral to a competent professional. My point at the moment is that active listening does not include the obligation of urging a patient to verbalize angry feelings, though it does involve accepting the patient the way she is: angry feelings, words, and all.

One of the distinct advantages of being a good listener is that you become very much more aware of the patient's feelings, problems, and concerns than you would if you yourself did all or most of the talking. When the time comes to read scripture, you are in a very good position to select a portion from the Bible which is related to the patient's needs. You are able to include in your prayer for her the specific matters she has been telling you about. Your reading and prayer will definitely be relevant instead of dealing in pious generalities that sound terrific but don't really speak to the patient's situation.

A by-product of attentive listening, a result which is by no means to be despised, is that it "buys" for the visitor a chance to say something important. Having had the pleasure of your ear for a time, the patient is much more likely to accord you the courtesy of listening for a while. She may even receive a word of advice, seriously consider it, and decide to act upon it — all because you first listened. A student once said to me, "I'm a good listener. I have no problem letting people talk. But what can I say to the patient? I have a feeling I ought to be able to *say* something too. "My answer is: listen, learn what the patient needs, and when "your turn" comes, share with her the word that you feel is appropriate.

The Limits of Creative Listening

It ought to be recognized that this active listening technique is useful only with patients who are able to *converse* and not merely to talk. There's a difference. Cabot and Dicks point out that there are three kinds of persons who cannot be helped through active listening, and I would add a fourth. The *first* we have seen, is the inveterate chatterbox, whose idea of conversation is one-way, from her to you. She talks on and on, but most of the time she avoids the real issue. The compulsive talker who hears not a word of your responses or, even if she does, pays no attention, cannot be helped much. Your ministry to her will probably be just to stay with her for awhile and show that you cared enough to come. Be prepared to converse, but if she clearly does not want a two-way conversation, listen passively for a short while, then take your leave as graciously as possible.

You might try the technique of gentle confrontation (described briefly in the next chapter). That is, you might say in a kind way, "Jane, you talk a blue streak every time I come. Are you doing it to avoid some subject?" Something like that. If she picks up the opportunity to talk about her apparent compulsion, a creative conversation might ensue. If not, don't spend all day trying. After all, only she can decide to change and benefit from your listening. When the time is nearly up, you could perhaps say a prayer, if you think she might appreciate it, and trust that the prayer at least might help. But only if you feel certain that she'd welcome it.

The *second* type of person who can benefit nothing from a ministry of creative listening is the unimaginative conversationalist. She can't think of what to say. So she offers nothing for you to listen to. She can respond briefly to your questions, your probings about her condition, her concerns, her feelings. But the conversation begins to sound like the game of Twenty Questions with the patient responding Yes or No. You try various ways of involving the patient but nothing gets her talking. Don't keep on for more than five minutes. If you get no significant response by that time, you can be fairly certain that the person hasn't the ability to converse. She may initially be afraid of you, and if so, your not pressing her is the best way to allay this fear. When she feels less threatened, she'll open up, perhaps on the next visit. If she is a member of some church, she may appreciate a prayer and a reading. But active listening will not work with her at the moment; so don't wear yourself out.

The *third* kind of patient who cannot make use of an active listener is the one who is very ill. A patient may have had a stroke and cannot talk. Another is just too weak, too tired. You don't help this kind of patient by trying to make her talk. She just doesn't have the energy or the ability. Don't force her to accommodate your need for conversation. You'll have to find some other way to minister to her. Once again, if she's a believer, she may appreciate a verse or two of scripture and a brief prayer, perhaps even a hymn. If you know someone well, just sitting quietly for a moment or two, perhaps in silent prayer, possibly holding her hand, may be the most appropriate kind of ministry. Or maybe she would like you to read a story or a letter from a friend.

A man I visited some years ago, *on a doctor's request*, just would not or could not speak to me at all. He was lying on his stomach with his head half buried in the pillow. I introduced myself. No response. I said that the doctor thought he'd like to talk to me. No response. I remarked that he seemed to be feeling really low. No response. I kept quiet, my hand gently on his shoulder. No response for awhile. Then I thought I heard him utter, "There's no hope." So I said, "You know God loves you, don't you?" No response. So I felt led to pray: "God, you know this man's burden and need. And I know that you love him. I pray that you'll help him. Take the weight of his burden and bear it with him. Please give him your peace. I pray in Jesus' name. Amen."

There was nothing more I could do. But the story had a happy ending. Next day when I visited, this person was sitting up in bed. His wife was with him, looking quite pleased. We had a brief conversation and another prayer. One thing led to another, and a long-term friendship developed which still includes some spiritual ministry and creative listening.

The *fourth* category of person for whom a listening ministry is useless is the one who does not want you there but is too polite to ask you to leave. You generally can tell by the look on the patient's face whether her silence comes from one of the three reasons already mentioned, or whether she's trying to freeze you out and give you the message that she's "not interested." The best thing to do is graciously back off and visit someone else.

Is it necessary to be a Christian to be a good creative listener? No, but I believe a Christian listener has the advantage over a non-Christian, because in his perceptions and discernments of patients' needs, he can bring to bear his additional awareness of the spiritual dimension of the human situation. It stands to reason that a patient who believes in Jesus Christ will probably derive more help from a

Christian visitor, because both patient and visitor share the same heritage and faith.

Nevertheless, if an unbeliever is a truly sensitive and creative listener, he can still be of considerable help to a believer. I know at least one Christian patient who was enormously helped by a non-Christian therapist, both to understand himself better and to see where he stood most in need of divine aid. Many people were praying for this person and also for his therapist. If we add our prayers to the efforts of the non-Christian therapist as we pray for the Christian client, we shall do well.

Sympathy and Empathy

It is useful to define empathy by contrasting it with another common human emotion — sympathy. It is easy to confuse the two. Often the one changes into the other, and at times both exist together. When a change does occur, the movement is most often from empathy to sympathy rather than the reverse.

Sympathy means being affected by or even having the same feeling as the patient has. If she feels like crying, you feel like crying. If she feels like celebrating, you feel like celebrating. If she's indignant about some cause, you are indignant with her. Sympathy can be a helping emotion, but very often, when tinged with pity, it can cripple a patient, weakening her courage, damaging her sense of responsibility, and fostering self-pity rather than a will to get better. When you feel and express emotions like the patient's, you support and encourage her suffering. The result is two cripples instead of one.

But sympathy does have its good points, and in some circumstances can help the other person. Without sympathy we would not be able to "weep with them that weep and rejoice with them that rejoice" (Rom. 12:15). Often a good cry with someone is "just what the doctor ordered," a point stressed repeatedly by Dr B. McNeel, former chief of psychiatry at North York General Hospital in Toronto. Jesus complained that neither the music of the dance nor the wailing of the funeral evoked any fellow-feeling from the people of his day (Luke 7:23). Sympathy is not *in itself* bad. It has a place in life. But there are times when it is completely inappropriate.

Empathy means entering into *(en)* the patient's problematic situation, grasping her viewpoint and its accompanying emotions, without being swept away or overly moved by the same emotions. If the patient is depressed, you can "get into her shoes," see the situation from her point of view, and understand how she feels. That's empathy. But if sympathy gets the better of you, you will soon be feeling depressed along with her. You'll end up "under the same rock"; then there'll be two depressed people instead of one. And what help can you be to her then? Empathy means to "be with" the patient "where she is" yet, at the same time, to "be yourself" and to minister to her out of your own strengths.

In his book *Giving And Taking Help* Alan Keith-Lucas suggests that the helper's imagination has a lot to do with his ability to empathize. The visitor can imagine how it feels to be in the position of the patient, and is able to communicate to her that he understands her feelings. Such an imagination is fired by Christian love. But it is an imagination that does not get sucked into the patient's emotional state to the extent that the visitor cannot stand back a little to help the patient to deal with herself.

Professor Keith-Lucas points out that sympathy is by far the easier emotion. He means, I suppose, that it's something one might enjoy or even wallow in. It takes no work at all. You just let it happen. Empathy, on the other hand, requires discipline, alertness, a constant focus on and ministry to the other person. It requires arduous learning about human needs in general. It means purposefully and systematically growing in knowledge of what people are like. Empathy comes into play regardless of whether one likes or dislikes the client. It's a serving function, performed with genuine but disciplined compassion — and always from the perspective of a helper who is constantly aware of whose problem it is (not the visitor's, essentially, but the patient's).

How The Patient Is Helped Through Creative Listening

The main purpose of the pastoral visit is to serve the patient, to help her according to her needs. Whatever change takes place comes from within the patient. It is not a change which the visitor produces by argument or persuasion. It is not a result of logical reasoning, though some logic may enter into it. How it takes place is ultimately a mystery to the visitor.

We leave the How to God and the patient. Christians believe in the work of the Holy Spirit and in the power of prayer. But we don't always act with faith. If we really believe that the Holy Spirit is at work all the time, we can be assured that he will lead both us and our patients. The Holy Spirit takes all that you do, together with all that the patient feels and thinks and does as you minister to her, and enables the patient to "change gears," to decide so imperceptibly that even she may not be fully aware of it. Only subsequent developments show what actually did happen. Of course, a change can be more evident, more dramatic and sensational, but not usually.

You may get no credit at all. We don't become pastoral visitors in order to gain credit. We listen in Christ's name, and his Spirit does the changing. Sometimes we are privileged to see it and give thanks. At other times we have to be satisfied with the simple reward of knowing that we have followed the Spirit's prompting and done his bidding. What a relief to the pastoral visitor when he grasps this truth! He can visit the sick without any preplanned agenda, without any predetermined goal that he might feel compelled to attain. He can show love without having to guarantee the results of that love, without having to prove anything to himself or to others. When improvement does occur, the visitor can genuinely thank God for what *he* has done. And he can thank God for the privilege of being, even in his weakness and inadequacy, one minister among others — doctors, nurses, — who cared in both attitude and action. He is one of the treatment team whose love and skills, in God's grace, served a person in need.

5

How To Be A Creative Listener

There are many ways for a creative listener to respond to a patient in conversation. It will be helpful to list them here. By keeping such a list you can from time to time review your conversations with patients, and judge whether you're (a) getting into a rut by offering the same sorts of responses over and over again, regardless of appropriateness, and (b) whether you're gaining skill in tailoring your part of the conversation to the real needs of the patient. Many of these ideas I owe to Dr. Howard Clinebell (see list of recommended reading).

Various Listener Responses

1 One useful kind of response is *challenge*. "Well, then, what do you think you'll do about this?" or "Have you made a decision yet?" or "Look at all these resources you have. Have you thought of how you are going to use them?" or "How will you adjust to your work situation now that your leg is gone?"

2 Then there is *confrontation*. This is not, as some people mistakenly suppose, a matter of opposition or belligerence. It involves facing a person with the reality of his or her behavior or attitude, and usually it's done very gently. "Do you realize what you sound like?" (to a complaining patient). "Do you think you can move the clock back?" (to one who fantasizes).

3 Though all your relationships with the patient are carried on, it's to be hoped, with empathy, there is a response which could be called *understanding*. It shows that you are really trying to be with the patient where she is, to realize what she feels, to appreciate her point of view and all the contributing factors.

4 Then there's the *supportive* response, which shows you accept her the way she is. It could be called an *accepting* response. You reassure her that you accept her feelings, negative as well as positive. "It's OK to feel that way. I'd feel like that myself if I were in your shoes." You let her know you're "pulling for" her. You

encourage her, show that you have confidence in her ability to meet the next challenge. Prayer too can be intensely supportive.

5 Some responses are *teaching* or *informative* responses. Clinebell calls them *interpretive*. Explaining the way of salvation at the appropriate time is a teaching response. Explaining it when the patient is not ready is a gesture out of place. Telling what the Public Health nurse can do or outlining briefly the work of the Multiple Sclerosis Society are teaching responses. So is any explanatory word about the meaning of a fear the patient has, or of some false guilt that she feels. I would never suggest that you get into the role of an amateur psychologist. If you feel yourself getting in too deep, you can use a teaching response to say you're not a psychologist but the problem might be brought to a professional. Such advice as, "Why don't you ask your doctor what he thinks?" could be classified as a kind of teaching response.

6 From time to time you may express your *judgement* or *evaluation* of the patient's words or behavior. "Good for you!" or, "I'd be cautious about getting into that," or, "That's the spirit!" Your response may be longer, but basically you let the patient know how good or bad, wise or unwise her action appears to be, according to your personal assessment or even according to generally accepted standards or procedures.

7 At times you will find that you need to *probe* for information — about marital status, children, home situation, past experiences — information which, if the patient is happy to give it, can help you understand her better. Do guard against giving her the "third degree." You can probe gently and appropriately without sounding like an interrogator or a history-taking intern. Beware of probing just to satisfy your own curiosity or to gratify your prurient appetite.

8 Finally, a useful response to make when a patient is using your help to make a decision or solve a problem is a *summary of alternatives*. Usually the alternatives will be those that you have heard the patient mention during the conversation. Or you may tentatively suggest adding another alternative to the patient's list. When things get complicated and the conversation bogs down and seems to get nowhere, such a summary of the alternative courses of action can be very useful in pulling things together, and may even open up new avenues of thinking that had not come to mind before. "Well, now," you might say, "let me summarize what

you've come up with so far. You could do A or B or C and I might add that perhaps D is something you could consider too. Does any of those strike you as the one you'd prefer to follow?"

The above list describes quite a variety of listener responses. After you've been visiting for some months and can take a fearless look at yourself with the help of the group or team, you may discover yourself to be very good at certain of these responses and very sparse with others. That discovery may kindle within you a new eagerness to try some of those other responses in appropriate settings and thus add to your creative equipment and skill.

Words and Feelings

In all aspects of creative listening it is wise and realistic to assume that *Words* alone are not the most significant communication that the patient will send your way. A good rule of thumb is always to have your antennae out for feelings: the feelings behind the words, feelings which may not correlate at all with the words being uttered. A rather obvious example of this is when you say "How are things going today?" And the patient says "Just great!" Does she say it with genuine enthusiasm, with sarcasm, or as a habitual response which her depressed demeanor belies? Your response should reflect the mood that comes across, not just the words.

Another kind of example related to this topic comes from Job 6:26. Job asserts that the words of a sick and upset man must not be taken too literally. He pleads with his "comforters" to pay less attention to the way he expresses himself and more to the pain and anguish which suffuse his words. We too, when we are visiting, ought to respond to the person's true feelings, and not allow such things as violent language and swearing throw us off. Were we to react negatively to bad language by our facial expression, or respond with a self-righteous rebuke, our attention would be deflected from the patient's real need. And worse, our reaction could stifle her and leave her worse off, with her negative feelings all bottled up inside.

One negative feeling you may often hear, or may often sense in a person who's afraid to say it out loud is *Why?* Why has God let this happen to me? What have I done to deserve this? Why is God punishing me? It is tempting at such a time to give a little sermon to justify God's ways with man. But usually the patient won't be able to hear it. She's not in a rational "space." At the moment she's all emotion. What she needs is your response to the agony behind her words. Your nearness and support will mean more to her than a hundred sermons. The practical assurance of a hand on her shoulder, a simple reply "It's hard to take," "It's so hard to understand," or some other response that catches her feeling and shows that you understand and accept her. This is her deepest need at the moment.

After the immediate strong feeling subsides, the patient herself may come up with her own answer. It often happens that way. Or she may ask what the Bible has to say about it. She may not ask at all but may put out silent signals that she'd like to know more. If so, you can cautiously introduce the subject.

The Visitor, a Counselor?

From the previous discussion it may seem that a hospital visitor must also be a pastoral counselor. Readers might react to this supposition in a variety of ways. One might feel that such an expectation is beyond the reach of any lay person's capabilities and conclude that he's unfitted to be a competent pastoral visitor. Another might be falsely encouraged to attempt more than he is capable of, and assume a role that only a professional counselor ought to adopt.

Surely the truth lies in being aware of one's limitations and capabilities and acting accordingly. What is counseling, after all? There's a real sense in which we do it every day, whenever we talk with anyone about any problem. Basically it is helping another person to solve his or her own problem. It is a two-way process that a pair of mothers might engage in over the back fence when discussing discipline in the home or the difficulties of dealing with a bad teacher. The answer to how much counseling the lay visitor should do is never to go beyond your competence. Be a creative listener, that's the basic ministry. It is just one person ministering to another, using whatever experience and gifts that he has. The only danger would be if a vistor set himself up as an accredited counselor, or paraded himself as having expertise and authority that he does not have. It would be illegal as well.

6

The Visit Itself

In this chapter, we bring together briefly some points already covered, and then go on to provide a fairly extensive list of "do's" and "don'ts," some practical guidelines for the visitor's behaviour in the sickroom. Most of them are pure common sense. They summarize and exemplify the basic principles of sick visiting that we have been considering.

1 Do *be clear about your purpose in visiting.* If you don't have a purpose or a clearly defined goal, you won't adequately realize exactly what you're trying to do. And when you're finished, you won't know whether you achieved your goal or came anywhere near it.

I believe there should be two main goals for any visit—an *ultimate goal* and an *immediate goal.* I don't know what your ultimate goal might be. My own is something like this: "Wouldn't it be great if this person trusted Jesus Christ and had such an intimate relationship with God that she would allow the Holy Spirit to help her become what she was created to be." You or I alone cannot bring this goal about. We are co-workers with God, and we put our faith in him. Your immediate goal will vary with the person you visit. For me, and possibly for you, the following statement encompasses the common element in all immediate goals: "To love this person in the name of Jesus," or alternatively, "That Christ may love this person through me."

2 Do remember to minister to *the patient's needs,* not to your own need to talk, to be liked, to show what you know, or to achieve success.

3 Do relate warmly to the patient, person to person, not as though she were merely a target for your ministry,

4 Know well the physical layout of the hospital. Try to be included in a general orientation tour if you can. It will help you feel more at home in the institution.

5 Try to get introduced to the nursing staff and orderlies if at all possible. Positive feelings and good rapport with them, even though they're far from close or intimate, will pay off.

6 Before the visit find out all you can about the patient: her age, marital status, family circumstances, reason for admission, whether she's from out-of-town. Everything does not hinge on this, but it helps greatly. You can find out quite a bit from the patient's nameplate at the nursing station, if you're allowed to look at it.

7 Before going in, do pray for the patient yourself. The prayer suggestions for your immediate goal (mentioned in number 1) provide a guideline for this pre-visit prayer. Like Saint Paul, you can pray without ceasing before, during, and after the visit—seeking a wordless contact with God in the back of your mind while you are ministering.

8 Pause at the same time to recall God's presence in and around you as you stand on the threshold of the room.

9 Consciously make a break with the moods and problems of previous visits, of home, or of any other involvements. Consciously ask, after leaving the previous activity and before approaching the door of the patient you're about to visit, "Now, what was going on back there?" Then answer your own question, commit the whole matter to God's keeping, and forget it for the time being. Go to the next patient, and trust God to help you be with her one hundred per cent.

10 Recall that you are part of a healing team. Others, because of ignorance or experience, may not know that you are on the team. But you must consider yourself as such, regardless.

11 If the door of the room is open, pause outside and survey as much of the room as you can see. Is the coast clear? Is a nurse or doctor doing something with the patient? If so, wait or visit someone else first. Is the curtain drawn? It may mean that the patient is undressed or on a bedpan. If in doubt, you can always check with a nurse. Look for flowers, cards, and other mementos that may indicate the number of friends and visitors this person has or does not have. You can complete this "survey" during the visit itself. It tells you something about the patient.

12 Knock before entering, even if the door is open. It gives the patient a chance to "cover up" if necessary, and prevents many embarrassments.

13 After knocking move in *slowly*. By this means you avoid stumbling over anything. This way you can also take in more of the pa-

tient's appearance and surroundings. And, more important, you can easily back out with an apology if your entrance was inappropriate.

14 Do find out ahead of time which bed your patient is in, and go directly to that bed. You can visit with other patients afterwards, if you have time. This avoids the other patients' feeling disappointed or rejected when you excuse yourself and move on. Trying each bed until you find the right one may detain you for so long that your time for the one you are supposed to be visiting will be severely limited.

15 Do train yourself to be observant of the patient in the first few seconds of your approach. Notice the expression on her face *before* she realizes who you are or that you've come especially to see her. Is her expression happy, contented, depressed, painful? What do you see on her nightstand? A Bible, other books? Do not worry if you miss something. It helps to notice things immediately. They all convey information about the patient. But all does not stand or fall with your initial observations.

16 Be ready for any sight, smell, or sound. Have your mind set to meet the patient herself beneath what could be very repulsive outward appearances.

17 Don't chew gum. It turns some people off!

18 Don't pick your nose or your teeth. (This has been known to happen.)

19 Don't suck candies or munch chocolate from the nurse's station.

20 Be careful about your grooming, body and breath odors, and tone of voice. Make sure your hair is neat, and if you have a beard, trim it tastefully. Sick people have a heightened awareness of such things. Loud voices grate on the ears. Speaking too softly strains the patient's hearing. A frowsy appearance is insulting. Strong perfume and the smell of tobacco on clothing or on the breath are taboo. I recall during a four-month illness of my own in a mission hospital in India how even the smell of cooking (food that I really liked) nauseated me terribly. So avoid the olfactory insult.

21 Greet the patient, and introduce yourself right away. Don't keep her guessing. Sense during this time if you're welcome.

22 Do not lean over the patient like a dentist. It may disgust or alarm her.

23 Sit or stand so that the patient can easily see and hear you without strain.

24 Be genuine. Do not act, prevaricate, or be phony. If you catch yourself assuming a "compassionate visitor's voice" or saying too often, "You look great" (when in fact she looks awful) or putting on a performance to meet some personal criterion rather than discerning and responding directly to the patient's need, then it's time for you to do some soul-searching.

25 Decline to give medical advice or opinions. This may become a temptation for you, especially if you've spent years at this ministry and are well read on health matters. But it's not your field. There's too much that you do not know. Not even doctors themselves discuss things with another doctor's patient. The answer to every medical question is: "The doctor's the one to ask."

26 Avoid discussing the value of a doctor's diagnosis and treatment. If the patient expresses mistrust or disappointment, urge her to talk with the doctor. Sometimes patients say that when the doctor comes they can't remember their questions and complaints or that there's no chance to talk because he comes and leaves so fast. In that case the patient may be advised to write her questions on paper as they occur to her, and to raise them immediately when the doctor arrives. The patient has a right to change doctors if she feels she must. Most people are afraid to do this, but don't advise every disgruntled patient to switch. It may not hurt at appropriate times, if a patient is terribly upset about her doctor, to inform her that she does have that right, and ultimately the decision is hers. This action would be appropriate mainly when the patient in her own mind has already "discharged" the doctor and feels stuck in an impossible situation. It is generally very inadvisable for you to criticize a doctor or discuss with a patient the value of his treatment.

27 Don't let moral faults (about which you can do nothing) repel you from the patient. A person in great mental and physical distress, finding you a good listener, may reveal personal matters that could shock you if you were not prepared. If you show shock or disapproval, you'll offend the patient so badly that your opportunity for ministry will be lost.

A girl may confide in you that she's just had an abortion. Someone may reveal that she and her husband are living common-law. You may hear admissions of business cheating, of illegitimate children, of shady occupations. The key to your response in all such situations is to focus on what the patient seems to be feeling or needing. If a girl says, "I'm going to have an abortion," and seems to wait for your response, you can say, "You seem to need to tell me that. Why did you want to tell me?" Keep probing for her need, and minister to that. If the patient wants to know what you feel or believe, or what the Bible says about it, you have to tell her, but not until you're sure that's what she really wants.

28 Don't stay too long. For the patient's sake err on the side of brevity, but don't act in a hurry to get away. About fifteen minutes is an average visit. Leave when the conversation is obviously over, even if it's very short. Stay half an hour if the patient really wants to talk and seems well enough. You have to play this by ear. There comes a time when, despite your feeling that there's still a lot to talk about, you have to say, "Well, I really must go now. I'll come again on Tuesday, and we can talk again if you like." There are other patients, of course, with whom you'd stay for only three minutes or even less. It is surprising what even a brief visit from an understanding visitor can mean to a patient. The very fact that you show your face is a sign of caring. I have often been told, long afterwards, about brief visits I've made and how much they were appreciated.

29 Avoid crippling sympathy (see chapter 5).

30 Generally make it a rule not to sit on the patient's bed. You may jar the patient or hurt her. She may have a broken hip. There may be a tube or a bedpan under the covers. The bed is the last bit of territory the patient can call her own. Respect it. Sometimes it does become necessary to sit on the bed in order for you to speak confidentially, or for the patient to see you easily. But never do so without the patient's permission or invitation. Another reason for not sitting on the bed is that your clothing may leave germs on the bedclothes or carry the patient's germs from room to room.

31 Avoid making excuses for your guilty feelings about not visiting earlier, or for other personal deficiencies or omissions. Don't burden the patient with your need to hear her forgiving reply. When you start doing this, the focus becomes reversed and the patient is forced to minister to your guilt. That's not what you're there for.

32 Do not raise depressing or alarming topics with the patient. Imagine the effect, on a patient who has been watching the dark and rainy weather for a week, of a visitor who exclaims, "What awful weather! I hate it!" Earthquakes, floods, accidents, murders, unemployment, and your own troubles are depressing topics to anyone.

33 Though it is essential to allow the patient her own feelings, don't encourage her to indulge in feelings of persecution. Be lovingly firm about this. It is not good for her.

34 Don't try to be an amateur psychotherapist.

35 Don't engage in a whispered conversation with a nurse or relative anywhere near the patient or outside her door. Even if you're not talking about her at all, she might think you are.

36 Don't say anything near a comatose or unconscious patient that you would not want her to hear. The hearing faculty seems the last to go, as patients who return to consciousness have confirmed. Assume that the patient can hear all you say. Assume she can hear your prayers and readings of scripture too. Never omit a prayer just because the patient is in a coma.

37 Never allow a patient's apparent insults or outrageous comments to affect your attitude toward her. Remember you're dealing with a sick person. Be charitable; don't take it personally. And above all, don't take revenge by not going back to visit her.

38 Don't play favorites. Naturally, if you have a large number of people to visit, you have to make a priority list. However, it is easy to put an unpleasant person at the end of the list day after day, so that the possibility of reaching her remains constantly slim. The antidote is to put her first on your list the next time around.

   We have to face the fact that some people are unpleasant or awkward to visit or you have to raise your voice for deaf people. Manipulative people can make you feel foolish and inadequate, especially when other patients and staff are watching. Don't penalize such persons by avoiding them.

39 Avoid arguing and debating with patients, unless you have a patient whose greatest need and obvious pleasure is to be diverted and entertained. Be careful, though, not to disturb the other patients.

40 Church and community news is OK in its place, but avoid gossip which can become negative and edged with malice.

41 If a patient seems unduly lethargic, mentally dull, confused, or thick of speech, do not jump to alarming conclusions about her condition. Check with the nurse; it may only be the effect of medication which in time will wear off.

42 When feasible, say you'll call again and give the date; then keep your promise! The patient's anticipation of your visit may be as enjoyable as the visit itself, and it increases motivation for healing.

43 If a nurse or doctor suggests only a brief visit, or makes any other suggestion, be sure to follow it.

44 Wear different clothing for each visit if you can. This may not be as easy for men as it is for women, but you can alter combinations of ties, shirts, slacks, and jacket or sweater. Variety brightens up the day. Even different kinds of little gifts and favors (if you like making such things) can bring some cheer. Leaflets, booklets, pictures, poems too, introduce welcome variety.

45 If the patient is on the mend, gently challenge her with what she's going to do from now on. It is good (as Cabot and Dicks suggest) to fortify the hope of a patient during long slow recovery by talking about her future. It may also help the patient who's acquired handicaps to think through how she'll manage them at home.

46 Always maintain confidentiality.

47 If you take the patient's hand, take it gently. Don't squeeze or shake it. You may hurt her.

48 Don't regale the patient with stories of your own illnesses and operations, or those of your relatives and friends.

49 Think ahead about the following situations and consider what you might do, so that in the actual situation you won't be caught short.

a If the patient knows no English (suggestion: use sign language, sign of the cross for blessing if you know she's Christian, and show goodwill by your demeanor).

b If the patient can't talk (suggestion: tell her to squeeze your hand for Yes but do nothing for No, or a quick eyeblink for Yes and a long one for No. She may be able to nod or shake her head as a signal.

c If the curtain is drawn around her bed (suggestion: ask the nurse).

d If she has visitors (suggestion: say, "Mrs Jones, I'm from the chaplain's office. I see you have visitors now; so I'll come back another time. Goodbye." She and the visitors may insist that you stay. Play it "by ear" from then on).

e If other patients join in your conversation (suggestion: include them, and if you pray, pray with them together. However, if there's something private to talk about, draw the curtain after courteously explaining to the others or take her to a quiet spot in a lounge or get permission to use the nurse's office).

f If she seems to be on a bedpan under the covers but you're not sure (suggestion: make the visit brief but courteous, and say you'll be around again).

g If she's lying uncovered, partly or entirely naked, and unaware of it (suggestion: stay cool, it's only her body. Just excuse yourself for a minute, if she's aware of you, and tell the nurse. Come back again when the coast is clear).

h If she asks you to take her to the washroom, to help her sit up, or to fetch something for her such as food or drink (suggestion: say, "the rules permit only nurses and orderlies to do that; I'll call one for you").

i If a patient seems to be choking, turns blue, goes into cardiac arrest be *sure* to get the nurse immediately. Don't worry about being proper. If necessary even shout for one. Make sure someone comes. A life may be in danger. You may even have to be spectacular or demanding, and risk looking stupid. But do it!

j If a patient wants to show you her operation, graciously decline, but if she pulls up her hospital gown and shows you before you get a chance to do so, acknowledge her gesture and "play it cool." This is easier if you are the same sex as the patient, of course.

k Summary: think ahead about what you'd do, and when it happens don't panic. When in doubt, you can always ask a nurse.

50 Don't get into the habit of using prayer as a formal routine way of saying goodbye or getting away.

Is all this a lot to remember? There's more! You'll never be able to learn it all at once. It's a good idea for the visitor to keep a notebook and write down things that happen, then check out the guidebooks and textbooks for suggestions. Gradually ideas add up and get stored away in the mind to be called on when needed.

7

Your Pastoral Notebook

Throughout this book I often stress the need for a visitor to learn, grow, and gain skills for his ministry. He does this by reflecting regularly on his experiences and trying honestly to perceive his own strengths and weaknesses, taking definite prayerful steps both to confirm those strengths and to overcome areas of personal deficiency. This kind of self-evaluation brings systematic direction into what otherwise might be quite random growth. The visitor looks at himself in relation not only to patients, but to other people and God. He examines his whole being—personality, character, knowledge, ability. This evaluation, though it grows specifically out of the visiting situation, has an inevitable relevance to all that one is and does.

No one should make this exercise too ponderous or "heavy". It is important, but that does not mean it must be doleful or exacting. It's an activity to delight in for the improvement of one's ministry, much as an amateur singer or instrumentalist might listen to tapes of himself and pay attention to listeners' comments to guide his practicing schedule. It's done for love; it's done with enjoyment. But it's work, nevertheless.

A most valuable tool for self evaluation is the notebook. From the very beginning, specialized training for institutional chaplains requires keeping verbatim notes of certain visits each day. Notekeeping can help lay visitors too. Chaplains in training have to write down entire conversations! But most lay visitors don't have time for this. They have other jobs and do visiting in their off hours. So it seems overly burdensome to insist on verbatim reports. However, notes are essential.

Let's begin by looking at the way notes can be made and kept. The important thing is to write down your notes immediately on leaving the patient. Go to a quiet spot, perhaps to the desk in the nursing station if you feel welcome there, or in the lounge, and jot down as fast as you can the important things you remember from the visit. Don't worry about neatness at first. With time you'll develop your own shorthand and timesaving methods for recording vital information.

I suggest copying these notes later into a looseleaf notebook that's easy to carry around with you. You may eventually decide to make your notes directly in that book. When for any reason (such as discharge from hospital) you stop seeing the patient, you can remove the page or pages and file them for future reference. You never know whether in future years you'll see that person's name again in the list of patients in the hospital, or hear that she's been readmitted. Maybe she'll even ask for you. Having the notes available on file will help you to recollect things about her so that you can talk as an old acquaintance.

You will want to record your first impressions of the person (how she looks before she notices you and begins to "play the host"), significant things that she said or you said, information about her family or friends, what you learned about her feelings and problems, what you learned about yourself. Quickly write down as much as you can remember. Don't hesitate over things you can't recall— they were not significant enough to impress you. As you get accustomed to this technique of notewriting, you'll find yourself naturally remembering more and more, and growing in awareness of what is significant enough to be noted down. One caution: do not worry about your notebook during the visit. Forget everything else but the patient. Afterwards you'll remember what's important for your ministry to that person. If you remember very little, don't despair. Just write it down immediately. Then go to the next patient.

I like to get visitors started on note-taking by providing some guidelines on a "log-sheet." Some weary of this sheet after a time, because they want to recall certain things and the log-sheet intrudes. However, I still recommend that after making notes without the log-sheet you go over the questions on it to see whether they trigger any further memories that might fill out your "diary" of the visit. Here is a copy of the log-sheet.

Log-Sheet for Lay Visitors

1 What information did you gather about the patient before the visit?

2 What were your first impressions about the patient and his or her room?

3 How did you first approach the patient?

4 How did the patient react to your approach?

5 What happened then?

6 Who did most of the talking? Why?

7 How long did you stay? Why?

8 What do you now know about the patient's feelings, problems, anxieties, attitudes, beliefs, family, work, etc.?

9 Describe briefly how you came to know the information in 8.

10 If you talked about religion, or God, how did this come about?

11 If you prayed with the patient, how did it happen and what did you pray about? Why did you feel it was appropriate?

12 In your opinion, where is the patient at this moment emotionally, psychologically, theologically, and in her personal relationship with God?

13 Were you to have an opportunity to visit this patient again, what approach would you take, and what things do you think he or she would want and need to talk about?

14 What did you learn about yourself in this visit? About your own personality? About your own emotional and learning needs?

15 Other comments.

Making notes like this may seem tedious to people who are eager to get on with visiting. If you're the kind with a need for high achievement, who's interested in totting up a good score (fifteen visits today, the most yet!), then notekeeping will not appeal to you. However, if you're concerned to grow both as a person and a minister, be content to visit fewer people in the beginning, and give serious attention to your notes. With experience the notemaking will become easier. It's great self-training discipline for the starter, and especially useful when the notes are used in team discussions and prayers.

Notekeeping has other advantages. Imagine going to the hospital three days later or next week, finding some of the same people still on your visiting list, and trying to remember, "Now, was that the one whose husband left her, or is that the one whose husband died? What did we talk about last week, anyway? Is this the one with cancer or heart disease, or the one with bad ulcers and dizziness? Is she the one-time believer who's really turned off the church, or the one who asked me to pray?" If you have notes to consult, you won't go in "cold," you won't make a *faux-pas*, and you can take up with your patient from where you left off. You'll remember her family situation, her problems, her interests, or matters she shared with you about her occupation. She'll be delighted you cared enough to remember.

Notes can also act as prayer prompters for you. When you pray at home, a glance at the notes will enable you to pray for a patient's specific needs. You don't need to have regular prayer sessions using notes from your visits, though it's not a bad idea. You could make each patient a subject of prayer, even as you write up the different ones you visit. Looking over these notes at home gives you a chance to reflect also, quietly and without pressure, on the significance of various reactions of the patient. The conversation was going fine when suddenly, according to your notes, she "clammed up." Why? What had you said just previously? Who had come in? Was she speaking of a memory too painful to recall for much longer? On reflection you may come to understand your patient a little better, and if not, at least you can open the matter to God in prayer.

You can meditate on the reactions *you* had during the visit too, and try to understand your own feelings and attitudes better. Often these are quite hidden from us until we start to ponder, preferably with the help of understanding colleagues on the team, the way we seem to affect other people in our conversations with them and how we let them affect us. Thus you can begin to understand and to deal with your own feelings. This is very important. As you go over the interview, those feelings, particularly the negative ones, which during the visit you had to keep under control for the sake of the patient, can safely come to the surface. You can experience them again, feel them freely, and bring them out in the open before God. You may have felt revulsion at the person's disease. Acknowledge it and tell God how you feel. Don't try to be "nice" about it. Express your emotions to him, confident of his understanding and acceptance. I do not suggest that you cultivate negative feelings. Acknowledge them and, when feasible, bring them to the group as well, or to a friend or to your minister. This will help you to be more aware and accepting of yourself and to be more humble in assessing and dealing with others.

As you recall the feelings you had but were obliged during the visit to suppress, you can begin to discover whether negative feelings blinded you to things the patient was saying or to cues she was giving. You can consider whether you let those feelings influence your reactions to her. This process won't take away the old feelings completely. The "old man" is always in us (Rom. 7), but the "new creature" will win (2 Cor. 5).

When writing or reviewing your notes at home you can give vent to your feelings. I do not believe that it's possible for us to remember feelings dispassionately. I cannot easily ponder the record of my visit in as cool a manner as I might someone else's report. If you don't feel things again when you go over the visit, one of two things is probably happening: (a) either you're still repressing your real feelings, not acknowledging or allowing them to surface, or (b) you weren't really "with" the patient and you need to consider whether your visit was a real ministry or a mere performance, the acting of a part.

You can use the writing of your notes as a "growth check" on yourself. Do you tend to use the same old responses again and again? Are there points in the conversation where alternative kinds of responses would have been more suitable — a challenging response instead of an understanding one, a teaching response instead of a judgment or evaluation? Do you need consciously to try some new responses? Are your perceptions and discernments limited by the same old blinkers? Do you need to do more reading or take more training? Is there something about yourself concerning which you should perhaps ask the group's opinion or seek their help — areas in your ministry where you possibly need to change? Such questions and probabilities occur to you both as you write up and meditate on your notes, and also as you discuss them with others.

One more point I would like to make about the usefulness of notes. As you type them up or ponder them at home, you'll find the exercise becomes an imaginative and creative adventure. Ideas seem to pop up from nowhere. "Why, of course, that's what she really seems to need . . . *Now* I see how she felt . . . *Now* I know what I should try to do . . . I think I should suggest that she contact the Senior Citizens' Club. Maybe I should put a church group in contact with her or ask her if she'd mind the minister calling on her."

You get flashes of inspiration as you relive the experience. You begin to see too, just how the patient is bearing her illness: perhaps as a punishment from God, perhaps as a result of her own life-style (about which she's now feeling guilty), perhaps as a temporary setback, a major obstacle to the achievement of the life goals, or perhaps even as an opportunity to reflect and grow. It's hard to pick up every nuance of feeling and attitude during the visit itself. But afterwards — with the help of notes, reviewing, pondering, prayerfully mulling things over — these ideas come. Then next time you visit, you can try some of them out. Gently put them before the patient, and if she takes them up, you may have a whole new experience of creative listening before you.

Here and there I've mentioned the group or the visiting team. Notes of your visits supply excellent learning material for the team sessions. As you discuss various points together, new learning needs will emerge. You can then plan together how to meet those needs: perhaps by studying some book together, by taking a course together, or by inviting a special speaker or resource person to help you. You may decide, for example, that you need to know more about the general needs of the terminally ill. You may need special information concerning the common attitudes and problems of heart patients. You may want some guidance in the use of a certain learning technique such as role-play.

As the visiting and learning team meets, other things may happen too. You may decide to pray together for one team member who specifically desires it, or for every individual in the group. You may decide to focus in prayer on a particularly needy patient that one of you has visited. Such team sessions can be very inspiring and edifying as well as practically educational. A new member recently told me that her first team meeting was a deeply moving experience. Notewriting is a most valuable tool for the visitor who takes his ministry seriously. It is valuable to himself and valuable to the whole visiting team.

8

Sharing The Good News

From time to time I have emphasized in these pages the need for the visitor always to be ready with a clear answer for the patient who asks him about God. I've maintained that the visitor's prime task is *not* to be an evangelist, but to be a creative listener. His ministry is to help the patient to decide for herself what she really needs and what she is willing to do about it. Every time I talk to students like this, however, the question arises, "But, how do I approach the patient as a *Christian*?" or "How can I convey the faith to the terminally ill?" or "How can I steer the subject to spiritual things?" The feeling underlying these questions is that any good social worker could probably do the kind of listening I've described, and most visitors want to be more than social workers.

How Listening Differs from Evangelism

It is undoubtedly true that some lay pastoral visitors are content to be there as Christian servants. Others are dissatisfied with that. They feel that somehow they must work in an opportunity to share the gospel message. "Woe is me if I preach not the gospel," they declare with Saint Paul (2 Cor. 9:16). If the visitor continues to be uptight in the patient's presence until he has had an opportunity to instruct her with the appropriate Bible verses, his anxious demeanor will spoil any possibility of being accorded a hearing. If the visitor were a good actor, he might be able to appear genuinely interested in the patient, but in that case his approach would be manipulative — controlling the conversation, forcing the subject by one trick or another. That is, he would be *pretending* to pay a visit and to focus on the patient, when all the time what he would be wanting is to preach. Saint Paul himself studiously avoided such a deceptive approach (1 Thess. 3–8).

My contention and my experience is that a Christian creative listener brings a different quality (not a different skill) to his listening than an ordinary social worker, in that he listens with an inner ear to the Holy Spirit. He is able, by God's grace and with practice, to minister to people in co-operation with that same Spirit and in humble confidence as a fellow-worker with God. Knowing the scriptures, he has a special source of wisdom to share with the patient, when the latter seems ready to receive it. Also he can pray. But he does not use these gifts against the patient's will. He knows that if he really respects the patient and listens, then those needs that originate deep in the spirit will emerge. It is up to the experienced visitor to learn how to detect that spark of incipient faith and to minister to it, so that if the Spirit moves the patient to ask, the visitor can take the opportunity to share the faith with her. People effectively and profitably learn only what they want and are able to learn. Jesus knew this. He said, "He that hath ears to hear, let him hear."

The opportunity for Christian teaching can occur in any number of ways. You may find yourself in a discussion with the patient on a theme that seems very important to her, out of which the question arises naturally. She might lead up to it by asking, "Do you believe in life after death?" She may engage you in eager conversation about a movie with a religious theme, a religious best-seller, or about religion in general. Any of these topics might be the setting in which you sense that the patient really wants to come to grips with ultimate questions. Don't jump to the conclusion that every time a patient raises these points she has this deeper desire. But she may.

In your listening you may hear ideas that express fear of death, the future, or sickness itself. Reflect back to the patient the message that seems to be coming through her words. Perhaps she's saying that she'd feel a lot better if she knew her life and future were safe in the hands of God. If she conveys apprehension or uncertainty be sure your response doesn't sound like an accusation or a judgment.

You may discern interest in the patient's request that you come to see her because she is very sick, or worried, or dejected, or when you've read a passage of scripture or prayed and she seems to want to talk about it. The question may surface while you and she are dealing with her plea to know *why*. Or she may have a friend who knows such peace with God that the patient wants what that friend has. How can she obtain it? She wants you to tell her.

Since you've been such a creative listener, the patient feels she can tell you anything. She might come to the point of asking you, "What must I do to be saved?" Perhaps the patient will indicate the same desire without actually putting it into a direct request. All that she says and does seems to tell you that this is what she wants to know.

When you're almost certain that it is, then you have to make it easy for this person to say so.

Two Listener Requirements

You need two things at this point. The one is to know what you're going to say in response to the question. The other is to be sure that the patient, who's now only strongly hinting, really does want to know. Let's deal first with what you're going to say.

When the patient asks a question similar to the Philippian jailer's, "What must I do to be saved?" (Acts 16:30), it is not time to fumble around. Nor is it a time to become academic. She doesn't need a theological dissertation. For the patient right now the answer has to be straightforward, clear, and relatively brief. Look at Peter's immediate reply: "Believe in the Lord Jesus Christ and you and your family will be saved" (Acts 16:31). The detailed teaching followed (verse 32).

For the patient this is a most delicate time. She's inwardly coming face to face with herself and her Creator. It's a time of turning, of changing the whole direction of life. The change may seem barely perceptible at the moment, but it will affect the patient's entire future if by grace she maintains the new course. It's a moment of accepting Christ's invitation through an act of will. It's a clear Yes to God's overture, a grateful response to God's own great act of personal empathy toward man by "getting into our shoes" in Christ. So keep the explanation clear. Keep it simple, and humble — one sinner telling another where he knows deliverance can found, one beggar telling another where there is bread. This moment is poor time to hesitate or to become embarrassed. What should a visitor say? He can share with the enquiring patient, in a manner appropriate to her needs and background, certain basics of the Christian faith. We're God's creation, highly valued, and though by sin we have "let him down," he cared enough to do everything necessary to reconcile us to himself. The price, which his son Jesus willingly paid, was the cross. The promise for those who believe, is forgiveness and restoration to an eternal positive relationship to the Father, sharing the risen life of Christ. In that restored relationship life is transformed and God's power is experienced in other ways. Appropriate scriptural assurances such as John 3:16–17, John 1:12, I John 1:8–9, and Matthew 11:28–30 add authenticity to the message (some readers will recognize here the "comfortable words" in the Book of Common Prayer). Many people want to make a prayer of commitment and thanksgiving in response to these assurances. The visitor can help a patient by letting her repeat such a prayer after him if necessary.

The other need for the visitor at this moment, which actually precedes the explanation of the gospel, is the need to make sure that the patient really wants to know what you think she wants to know. One way to ascertain this is rather simple, though it calls for much sensitivity. It is gently to confront the patient with what she seems to be saying. "As you talk, Mrs Jones, I get the impression that you'd like to be certain about God. Am I hearing you correctly?" Something like that. One may not come to the point of confrontation suddenly or even soon. If she responds, then you can feel reassured and continue. If not, you could possibly try again a little later. If she again fails to show interest, draw back — you've misread the cues.

You have to find your own way of probing. Sometimes I will say, "I guess we just have to hope and pray for everything to work out" — or some such innocuous comment. If the patient is on your wavelength, she'll likely agree. Then it's perfectly appropriate to say something like, "Do you pray much?" If she says yes, you could say something like, "I do too. What do you find yourself praying about most while you're here?" It's important to avoid controlling the conversation, though. You only begin speaking this way after your listening reveals an apparent interest. If she begins to balk at this stage, respect the new signals she now gives — signals that say, "I've had enough; please don't push me." You're there to minister and respond to her needs. If you respect them now, she'll gain confidence in you and may inquire again sometime.

You may well ask, "But what if I never see her again?" Well then, you've shown how a Christian visitor respects the inner sanctum of another's life, and she'll be less afraid of the next Christian visitor she meets. She may seek out some book, some radio or TV program, or better still, some church where she can hear and learn more. It happens all the time. Your ministry may have kindled a spark. The Holy Spirit is able to use someone else to fan that spark into a blaze.

The Gift of Helping

I have suggested that ministering to the patient according to her need, at the point where she is able to receive your help, is quite different from evangelizing. I think the special gift of the Spirit required for this type of ministry is similar to that of the pastor (Eph. 4:11), but probably most like that of the helper (1 Cor. 12:28). The visitor is basically a Christian *helper*. Something of the nature of evangelism or witnessing may take place within his ministry. However, if he begins on first contact to behave like an evangelist, he will no longer be a helper. He'll never minister to the patient at the point of immediate need, because he won't really know that need. Hospitals generally do not take kindly to evangelists. "No proselytizing" is the rule, even in denominationally endowed institutions. Yet evangelism and helping are both valid ministries. The Spirit distributes the ministerial gift to each as he will (1 Cor. 12:11).

The patient on the sickbed is a captive audience. She cannot walk away like the man who tires of the streetcorner preacher or the member of an audience who gets up and leaves. Before sharing the gospel, we *must* have *not only her full permission* (which might be given reluctantly out of politeness), we must discern whether she is *actively reaching out*. You can afford to wait. You can wait confidently because of two incontrovertible facts: (a) the human need for reconciliation with God is universal and real — we only wait for this to become the individual's felt need; and (b) there's no way you yourself by any skill, manipulation, or persuasion can create the spark of faith in anyone — it's the work of the Holy Spirit alone. All you need is to exercise your gift of *help* and be ready to show the way when the patient is moved to sincerely inquire.

What happens to people who respond in this way or who confirm a previous reception of Christ's gift and their commitment to him? In my own estimation, by far the best kind of follow-up a lay visitor can offer is personally, where appropriate, to introduce the patient to a prayer or study group in his own church, so that she can grow in the faith within the worshipping and serving fellowship of God's people. Often, however, the best you can do in the circumstances is urgently to suggest that the patient join a group somewhere. When there seems no possibility of this, and time presses, I sometimes give a pamphlet designed to guide a new or renewed Christian. A good one is put out by the church Pastoral Aid Society in England, entitled *The Way Ahead*. Some patients seem ready and eager to study the Bible and to memorize some helpful scriptures. I might give them the first book of a Navigator's Bible Study Course or introduce them to the Scripture Union Bible Reading Fellowship, or Canadian Home Bible League materials. Your own church may have suitable follow-up material that you could give to people at such times.

It is always a great joy to show the way of life to an eager pilgrim. It affirms the validity of the ministry of "helps" that I've stressed so strongly in this book.

9

The Use Of Prayer And Scripture

By now a couple of things are probably clear in the reader's mind. First, one does *not* go to the sickroom with a fixed agenda to read a portion of scripture or pray. At all times the needs of the patient as she sees them must determine the kind of approach and ministry suitable for any particular visit. A second point already made is that when scripture reading and prayer do happen to be appropriate, they ought not to be used as departure signals, so that "Would you like to have a prayer?" really means "It's time for me to go."

Often, however, a closing prayer is fitting and helpful. Pray out of your knowledge of the patient's specific situation. You'll know exactly what to mention if you've been listening. The prayers one often hears in church or those in the Book of Common Prayer or in other published books of prayers are not often suitable for the very personal ministry of the sickroom. Not that such prayers are less inspired or may not be used in appropriate circumstances. In the sickroom you experience an intimate encounter, and it seems fitting that the kind of prayer you offer be equally intimate: quite the opposite of liturgical. We might call it conversational, informal, or extempore prayer.

Even the Prayer Book prayers can be used in an intimate personal way by visitors who are not accustomed to leading in extempore prayer. There are prayers for special occasions which a visitor could adapt by adding the personal matters in appropriate spots. Here's an example using a prayer on page 54 of the Canadian Book of Common Prayer. It is a general prayer "for those in anxiety." A visitor could read this from the book, adding phrases such as I've placed in italics.

"Almighty God, who art afflicted in the afflictions of thy people: Regard with thy tender compassion those in anxiety or distress, *especially thy servant Mrs Jones who is concerned about where she's going to live and how she's going to manage to care for herself after she is discharged from hospital;* bear their sorrows and their cares; *it's good to know that you are near;* supply all their manifold needs; *especially Mrs Jones' need for an inexpensive apartment and help in cleaning and cooking;* and help all of us to put our whole trust and confidence in thee; *and we also pray that Mrs Jones will soon be well;* Through Jesus Christ our Lord. Amen."

To insert relevant matters from the conversation into the prayer, you would have to read it quite slowly, with deliberate pauses after each phrase, where you can insert your specific items of need. You may even be surprised, as you pause, to hear your patient add a word or two also. It has happened to me. Be ready for the day when some patient is so grateful that she spontaneously offers a short prayer after yours is finished, such as, "Thank you Lord for sending this visitor to me, and bless him as he goes to help other people too. It must be a draining work, and he needs lots of grace. Amen." You'll notice that the Prayer Book uses "thee" and "thou" and the visitor has used "you" in addressing God. If you get confused about such things and stumble around trying to be "correct," your prayers will sound like recitations. Good grammar is always appreciated, and no doubt one should practice to offer the Lord the best we have and also to show respect for those who hear us. But sincerity and relevance should have by far the highest priority in our prayers. Not even concern for good grammar should interfere with that.

One good thing about liturgical prayers is that they are couched in the traditional language of religion. It can feel very good to a patient to hear the familiar words, associated as they are with the community of faith and worship. They remind her that she is still part of the church, God's people. I believe the same is even more true of phrases from scripture. Familiar verses say far more to the heart of man than the mere words express. Thou art our refuge. . . the everlasting arms. . . nothing can separate us from the love of God. . . thou art our Good Shepherd. . ." This language is full of rich symbolism. Think of the stirrings of faith that could be aroused in the soul of a timid or insecure believer by such an opening as, "O God our rock, the secure anchorage of our souls. . ." Don't worry if you haven't a supply of such phrases just now. Between visits to the hospital do some reading, and perhaps introduce one into a prayer next time you visit.

In prayer we can acknowledge our limited human understanding of sickness, pain, and suffering. It is good to voice this, while expressing at the same time confidence in God's love, providence, wisdom, and trustworthiness. It's important to be honest. If God's ways in this specific situation are perplexing to your patient, say so. "God, there's so much we do not understand. There's so much that is so hard to bear. Help us to trust in your goodwill toward us. Like little children with a wise father we ask for what we need so much — (here mention the specific request). We rest now in your eternal and great love shown toward us in Jesus Christ. And we trust in your presence. Help us to trust you more."

There are times when we will not know what to pray about at all. A person is terminally ill. Should we pray for recovery or for grace to endure to the end? For cure or for patience and courage? When you don't know how to pray, you really have to be open to the Spirit. "Likewise the Spirit helpeth. . . and maketh intercession for us" (Rom. 8:26–27). I wish I could tell you what to say, but only the Holy Spirit can do that. It may be "God, we bring the whole situation before you — the pain, the illness, the hope, the treatment, and medication, all of it — and pray that you will provide what is needed for Mrs Jones' eternal well-being and wholeness." It may be something else.

Don't leave immediately, even if the prayer does seem to be the final phase of your visit. Pause for a moment. Give time for the person to say something if she wants to. Say something yourself if you feel it is right. Because what can happen, and often does, is that the prayer somehow opens up fresh longings or brings a new openness, a new honesty. So don't pray and run. Pray and stay — perhaps only for a moment, or if necessary, for a longer time. The need of the patient will be your guide, along with your intuition. Time may prohibit too long a stay. The patient, though she wants it, may be too tired. If that is so, you can promise to come again. And of course if you promise, keep your promise!

Some Christians who regularly minister to others develop other automatic routines besides using prayer as a departure ritual. There are those who just can't seem to shake the habit of always having to read a passage of scripture before they pray. There's no divine rule. Sometimes you'll pray without reading scripture. Sometimes you'll read or quote scripture without praying. The clue is what the patient's need suggests and what the patient seems to be ready for. But if the patient has asked you to visit her, knowing you're a Christian, or if during the conversation she happens to mention her church, past or present, or allude to the Bible or prayer, it is fairly safe to assume she'd like you to pray and/or read a passage. When in doubt, test the waters carefully (see chapter eight). Learn also to act on your inspired hunches or intuition. You may make a few mistakes in the beginning, but if you avoid aggressiveness and strive for sensitivity, you'll not likely do any harm.

If the situation seems to call for a couple of verses or a whole passage from scripture, the same principle applies: let it be appropriate to the patient's needs. At present you may have three or four favorite passages. Do use them, but begin to familiarize yourself with others. Here are some of the passages that I often use.

Romans 8:27–end — assurance of God's unceasing love.
Psalm 103 — God's forgiveness and power.
Psalm 23 — His strengthening presence and provision.
Psalm 121 — the Source of our help.
Psalm 37 — for the worrier.
Psalm 51 — for the penitent.
Psalm 91 — God's protection and care.
Psalm 34 — A celebration of God's aid.
Psalm 13 — A cry to be remembered and a song of assurance.
Psalm 104 — God's wonderful world.
Psalm 145 — Thankful praise and re-dedication.
John 14 — Encouragement to trust Christ for life here and hereafter.
Romans 5:1–11 — An affirmation of faith.
II Corinthians 4:16–18 — A focus on inner strength.
II Corinthians 5:1–9 — Comfort for the dying Christian.
I Corinthians 15:51–end — More comfort of the same kind.
Job 3 — Job asked "Why" too!
Psalm 44:17–end — So did the psalmist.

Sometimes I'll read a verse or two out of one of the Scripture Gift Mission booklets, which contain nothing but selected Bible verses. *Fear Not* and *Daily Strength* are two of their good booklets. After reading from one, I leave it with the patient, suggesting that other verses might also prove helpful to her.

We so often think of scripture as a teaching medium that I believe a word about one or two other uses may be appropriate. Seldom do I find that instruction from scripture is needed in the sickroom. The Bible can be a marvelous vehicle for the expression of feelings: need, adoration, or thanksgiving. Some of the above passages can also be read not to instruct or express feeling, but to remind, reassure, or encourage. Match the reading to the situation. Whatever blessings occur will result from the inner nourishment of soul and spirit, not from the accrual of academic knowledge. A fairly well patient may be interested in some Bible study or discussion of theology. But you won't find it so in most instances. The general idea is that, with the help of your presences and ministry, your patient "by comfort of the scriptures might find hope" (Rom. 15:4).

Prayer and scripture are two of the most tremendous means of grace a lay visitor can bring to a patient who has "eyes to see and ears to hear." As you grow yourself in understanding and knowledge of the Bible, you'll increase in the ability both to incorporate key phrases into your prayers and find just the right passage to read for a particular patient at a particular time. Of course you'll always be praying for the patient inwardly during your visit, as well as at other times. But as you increase in sensitivity and discernment of patients' readiness and needs, you'll learn when to pray aloud with her and when not to.

Prayer For Healing

What about prayer for healing? At the very least we ought to pray for the effectiveness of the treatment being given. I believe we should pray for wholeness of spirit, soul, and body too. There isn't space here for a treatise on healing prayer, but I am convinced that it ought to be a regular part of the therapeutic regimen for all who will accept it.

I suggest team prayer for healing where feasible. Let three or four people, including someone who loves the patient, lay hands on her as Jesus and his disciples used to do, and pray for her in the name of Jesus. Keep this up, silently if you wish, for five, ten, fifteen minutes. If you've ever been on the receiving end of such loving prayer, you'll know what a blessing it is, and how reluctantly you bear the removal of those hands. Repeat such prayer as often as you can. It's therapeutic.

Don't forget the sacrament of Holy Communion and anointing with oil in the name of Jesus. These are scriptural actions that convey the Lord's blessing for wholeness. Some churches commission lay persons to bring the sacrament of the Body and Blood. Recently I attended a Roman Catholic retreat where the priest blessed hundreds of bottles of vegetable oil for lay persons to use in anointing the sick at home, in the manner prescribed in James' epistle (chapter 5).

I do not believe in praying for wholeness with the rider, "if it be thy will." It is contradictory to do all we can with medicine and visiting to bring about a cure, and then in prayer to question the validity of our actions. Just because we don't know the explanation of apparent failures is no reason to refrain from asking for what we really want. We can't see the whole picture from God's perspective, but we do know that ultimately the restoration of all things is his purpose. Jesus encouraged us to pray for wholeness.

Prayer for healing is a large and fascinating study. There are many books written about it. Choose a reputable author or two, and learn what you can. Join your prayer effort with the doctors' treatment for the maximum possible approximation to wholeness for every patient you visit.

10

How To Visit
The Dying

Sooner or later the lay visitor will find himself in the presence of a person who is not going to recover from her present illness. And even though we have legitimate reason to believe in miracles, we have to face the fact that miracles can postpone death for a limited time. How will you minister to the patient whose death seems imminent? She may be in painful agony, she may be "drifting away," she may seem perfectly healthy. But all the signs say "no exit." How do you serve her? Consider, first of all, some of the situations you might run into.

Various Terminal Situations

One patient is fortunate enough to have a doctor who has been able with sensitivity and compassion to break the news that the disease is unlikely to give her much more time to live. The physician will promise to keep on trying, and to keep the patient free from pain. He may suggest that a minister of religion can do much more for the patient than he can. He may propose ways in which patient and family can make the best of whatever time remains. He may even be a man of faith, able to give that spiritual encouragement which will enable the patient to make maximum use of ministries like yours or the clergyman's. It's much easier to minister in a situation like this, because here the helping people can speak honestly, without being starkly factual or impersonally clinical. Together they can help the patient face reality without any pretense or anxious deceit. Everyone's energy can be channeled into creative use of time and resources for living out the close of a life.

Contrast this situation with that of a patient who, to the best of all medical knowledge, is "terminal," but to whom no one has conveyed anything but superficial information about her condition. There may even be a conspiracy to keep the truth from her. At times this strategy is necessary, in the doctor's opinion, because of the patient's apparent inability to receive and cope with the information.

However, it is difficult for any pastoral visitor to minister in such an artificial situation. Often there is an atmosphere of forced cheer and a constant effort to carry on as if all were "normal." Difficult as it may be for the pastoral visitor, he must realize that the people so affected still have needs, and that there is a ministry which he can offer.

The point to grasp here is that you yourself can expect some day to be ministering to a patient who does not know that her illness is terminal. Possibly everyone has been told but the patient. Often, however, the patient senses, sometimes with certainty, that the end is approaching. When I was very ill myself and nearly died, I could almost pinpoint the day when the physicians and staff began to think of me as a possible terminal case. But I didn't share it with any one. I kept it to myself and prayed. The patient may confide this feeling with you if she finds you an empathetic listener. And you can respond either to her outright requests or her "signals" inviting your support.

Death from sickness comes in different ways. You will meet patients who are dying very slowly. The diagnosis, for example, may be Hodgkins Disease, and death may be years away. Such people will probably be mentally alert and quite able to talk intelligently and at length about their life and its meaning. There are patients who have a rapidly progressing disease which is expected to take them within weeks or months. Some will be comatose for days or weeks. Here and there you'll meet a patient who takes suddenly ill, or has suffered a severe accident and has only days or hours to live. Others may linger in a state of complete mental confusion for weeks on end. Some patients have many relatives and friends. Others have few or none. Some have families that seem not to care. They are very alone.

You must meet each dying patient as a unique person. There is no "average" dying person. The key to your ministry to dying people is the same, essentially, as it is for anyone else: what are their needs? What kind of ministry are they able and ready to receive from you? Your ministry will be conditioned as much by the patient's self-awareness and receptiveness as by your scriptural knowledge, your understanding of people, and your ability to make it easy for her to talk to you. It doesn't *all* depend on you.

Facing Your Own Death

If you have faced your own death as an approaching reality, you will be able to help others who are struggling with their feelings and attitudes toward theirs. You will have a better idea of what the patient is going through, and will be less inclined to become frustrated with her, threatened by her fear and depression, or hysterically dogmatic in trying to impose rather than share your faith according to her readiness to hear.

Facing the reality of your own death does not mean mere intellectual acknowledgement of the fact that one day you will die. In order to be able to empathize with the terminally ill, you need to have felt the nearness of the Angel of Death yourself, and to have dealt with him. Saint Paul faced the sentence of death many times. He had not only an intellectual understanding, but also a "gut feeling" about what it is to despair of life. Your imagination can help you here. Ask God to help you feel what it would be like, right now, were you to be sentenced to death, were you forced to contemplate the severing of all relationships with people as you now experience them, especially those near and dear to you. Imagine being cut off from your interests, your work, the projects in which you have deep personal and emotional investments. Picture all the unfinished business; envision the plight of your family, their sorrow, and grief.

Or try another approach. Contemplate what it will be like when the dearest one to you is taken from you in death — the grief you'll experience, the mourning for one who will never come back, the enormous crater ripped open in your life. Then think of dying as losing not only one person, but losing everyone and everything, not by their demise, but by your own. Go through this exercise alone and as vividly as you can. That will be a beginning of facing your own death.

Maggie Kuhn, in Dieter Hessel's book about her, suggests that doing a "life review" and sharing it with someone is a good technique to help an individual face death. The method is to draw a horizontal line on a piece of paper. At the left end write the date of your birth. Somewhere along the line make a mark indicating where you are today, dividing the line into two sections. At the right end, note the year you expect to die. Then talk about it with others who've done the same exercise. Somewhere over the first section of the line write what you've done so far with your life, and over the second, what you intend to do with the rest of your life. Then share those things with the others. The exercise can be a great help in bringing home the realities of your own creatureliness and finitude, and of your own approaching death.

The date you were born.	Your present age and circumstances	The year of your death.

|---------------------------|---------------------------|

| What you have done with your life up-to-date | What you plan to do with the remainder of your life |

But, you say, I'm a Christian. I'm not afraid of death. I don't mean just your *fear* of death. Nor am I dealing here with Christian doctrine. I'm talking about your inner feelings. If you are in touch with your emotions, you'll be infinitely more helpful to others who are having similar experiences. Saint Paul did not hesitate to write about his deep feelings. He said that he would rather go to heaven to be with the Lord. But he wouldn't like to be "unclothed" in the process — that is, to be without a body. The possibility of losing his present body was most unpleasant to him (2 Cor. 5:1-4). Our very human Saviour himself had feelings. He felt the loss of his friends' support in Gethsemane when death was near. And though, in a way we'll never completely comprehend, he bore the terrible burden of humanity's sins, his physical pain on the cross being made infinitely harder when the Father seemed to have forsaken him (Mark 15:34) — even though he bore the agony courageously and manfully, we can detect, in his earlier conversation with his disciples, a desperate need of their presence and friendship. He had a reluctance to lose contact through death with those he loved so much. Surely his deep sorrow in Gethsemane was tinged with the same sadness that he had expressed earlier when he wept openly at the grave of his friend, Lazarus (John 11:35).

Our accepting by faith the atoning death of Christ does remove forever the fear of rejection by God. His resurrection inspires a sense of victory and a sure and certain hope. But the experience and prospect of death for us, as for Paul and Jesus, is still fraught with much sorrow and pain, even though its sting is removed (1 Cor. 15:54-57).

The Phases Of Dying

Dr Elisabeth Kubler-Ross, after talking with hundreds of dying patients, observed that they experience, generally speaking, five phases in the process of nearing death.[10] Briefly they are:

1 *Denial*. The patient cannot accept that the prognosis is true. There must be some mistake. "I know I'm going to die sometime, but not now." Dr Kubler-Ross sums it up in the exclamation, *"Not me!"* This denial stage is usually preceded by a short period of shock, numbness, a feeling of unreality, or reeling from the blow of the bad news.

2 *Anger*. This is anger at anyone and everyone or at life or existence in general. The focus of the anger may even be you; so don't take it too personally. It's a reaction to a very very deep hurt: "How could God or life or the hospital allow such a thing to happen?" The patient's whole being cries out, *"They can't do this to me."* The patient may ask *"Why me?"* This actually is less a demand that you justify for him the ways of God to men, than it is an expression of bewilderment and frustration and of fighting back. For you to say with sympathy, "It's really hard to take!" will be more useful to most patients at such a time than most theological explanations. There may be need for theology later, but in the midst of the person's agony of soul, the greater need is for a friend who understands and will stick by her. When Jesus needed friends in the Garden, he too in a sense asked "Why me? Is it really necessary for me to drink this cup?" Very often, if you minister with simple understanding and empathetic listening in such circumstances, you'll find that the patient will talk herself around to the place where she'll do her own thinking about God. When her emotion is less overpowering, she may even want to discuss the whole question of God and pain. At such a point you may be glad that you have read and absorbed a book like Philip Yancey's *Where Is God When It Hurts?*

3 The next phase is *bargaining*. That's when the patient begins to acknowledge, *"Yes, it is happening to me, but. . ."* The thoughts that follow that *but* could be many and varied. Some might expect, by following the doctor's instructions minutely, to buy an extension on life. Others might hope, by good works, to win from God a few more precious years. Some might return to a half-neglected prayer life, church attendance, Bible reading, or other religious practices. The kind of "bargaining" one does is a very individual and personal matter.

We must not, however, regard such bargaining as small-minded, hoggish, or demeaning. In a way Kubler-Ross's choice of the term *bargaining* for this phase is unfortunate because of the derogatory connotation we often give to that word. *Attempts at negotiation* might be better though more cumbersome. *Counter-vailing effort* is quite often in the patient's mind and motivation — that is, mustering all resources of God and man to hold off Enemy Death as long as possible and to score points against him. It's as though the patient says, "Yes, death is going to win out someday, but I'm going to do all I can to postpone that day!"

4 *Depression.* The patient finally seems to calm down and somewhat reluctantly or grudgingly acknowledges *"Yes. It's me. I'm dying."* She experiences a kind of *preparatory grief* for the many losses she will undergo. She may begin withdrawing from the interests of her life. Casual friends meet her emotional needs less and less, and cease deeply to interest her. She may weep a lot. She needs understanding and support, assurance of care, and a sense of being valued.

5 *Acceptance.* The patient's attitude now is, *"Yes, me! It's going to happen.* I'm not going to fight it any longer. *I'm ready whenever it happens."* Such acceptance, says Kubler-Ross, actually reduces the intensity of pain experienced by the patient. This fact has been documented at the Massachusetts General Hospital, where the amount of pain medication needed by patients with various attitudes toward death was closely monitored. Having someone near to understand and talk about things that are meaningful to the patient (not focusing on the pain itself) also reduces the pain. Philip Yancey quotes scientific experiments showing that a patient's pain threshold can be strengthened by 19 to 45 percent when his or her attention is diverted to other concerns and interests. Could this be the psychological reaction of the early Christian martyrs who were given special grace to feel no pain? Could it have been because their whole being was focused on the bliss that awaited them in heaven?

As death approaches, the patient often wants to see all her loved ones at least once more, and maybe even some of the places and things that have meant much to her. She wants to say goodbye to them. Toward the end she wants only those who are closest to her — husband, mother, brother, friend, or perhaps the nurse. If you don't seem to get through to her now as you used to, this is what's happening. Don't feel rejected. You can't be the most significant person in everyone's life. The family, however, will probably appreciate your continued interest. On the other hand, things may turn out quite the opposite. The patient may need you more than ever. There's a word for this gradual withdrawal from life — *decathexis*. You might use it in discussion with the professionals, but not with the family or the patient.

Other Needs Of The Dying

It will help to take note of seven further points about the phases people usually go through as they approach death. *First*, the attitudes of denial, anger, bargaining, and depression are psychological defense mechanisms which the patient needs in order to cope with her present situation. Do not make the mistake of trying to talk or argue a person out of these natural attitudes. For the moment, she needs whatever phase she is in just to hold herself together.

Secondly, throughout all the phases most patients cling to the *hope* that a cure will be found, that a turn for the better or a miracle will take place. The patient needs this hope. Do not smash it with arguments that she must face reality and accept the inevitable.

Thirdly, most patients experience a great deal of ambivalence between hope and denial, hope and depression, hope and acceptance. Thoughts and feelings swing up and down. Do not be surprised if the patient one day despairs of her situation and the next day is hopeful again.

Fourthly, the patient is likely to move backward and forward among the phases, or may experience two at once. She may be angry one day and bargaining the next. She may move out of depression into acceptance, and then back again into depression or even anger. On the whole the predominant movement is through the phases as Dr Kubler-Ross has delineated them. But there are always exceptions.

Fifthly, some patients get "stuck" in one phase and die in the midst of it. I recall one hospital worker who, until the day of his death, denied that he really had a serious illness. Although the doctor had never told him the truth, this man could easily have guessed what the diagnosis was. And he could have asked the doctor outright, if he had been emotionally able to do so. But he needed the defense mechanism of denial in order to cope, and he lived to the end in the midst of it.

I honestly feel that the doctor did this person no real favor by witholding the truth. I've seen other patients with less faith than this man, and with the same degree of emotional stability, move quickly and "successfully" through denial into anger, bargaining, depression, and acceptance because in the beginning the doctor did tell them. After the initial shock, they coped much better. We just have to accept the non-communicative doctor as one of the occupational hazards in the environment of our ministry. But let's not be too hard on him. He too has needs. We simply have to do the best we can within the imposed limits. Our attitude should be to hope, pray, and work for better communication among all members of the healing team.

Sixthly, a deep faith in Christ, the assurance of forgiveness, and the certain hope of the resurrection and eternal life, make a tremendous difference to the believing patient in the face of impending death. The late Dr Orville S. Walters, in the fall issue of the *Christian Medical Society Journal* 1975, observed that, as the day of his certain death from cancer drew near, he became increasingly aware that books like Kubler-Ross's *On Death and Dying* take little notice of the rich resources which the Christian faith provide for the dying believer. A competent psychiatrist, well trained and practiced in the skill and discipline of self-awareness, Dr Walters reported that he could not identify in his own experience the phases of dying delineated by Dr Kubler-Ross. He felt the reality of God's supportive and heartening presence at all times. His personal, vital, and intelligent relationship with God seemed to make it possible for him to accept approaching death with peaceful equanimity. He was able to go on counseling troubled people, commending them to the grace of God whenever he could appropriately and effectively do so.

My own experience of a brush with death through illness, and my contacts with other believers on their death beds, bear out the truth of Dr Walter's testimony. It seems to me that for a Christian the psychological stages or defense mechanisms are not so much bypassed, but rather they are swallowed up into a far greater and over-riding experience of the real presence of the One who is known personally as Redeemer and Friend. Quite literally, "Death is swallowed up in victory" (1 Cor. 15:54).

What then are we to say about the believer who, in spite of God's presence and assurance, seems nevertheless to experience anxiety, denial, depression? We must not pretend that these feelings are not there. Nor have we the right to pass judgment on any supposed paucity of faith. We minister to a believer, as to anyone else, with empathetic understanding. But there is this difference. For them the

Christian visitor can draw with enhanced effectiveness on scriptural resources, which both accept, and on the real presence of the Lord, whom both love and worship.

Try always to minister to the needs of the patient, even when that need appears to be to die soon. When a dying patient says, "I wish the Lord would take me home," or "I've had enough pain; I want to go," can you receive such a statement without having to contradict, to change the subject, to preach? Can you say those very things for her in a prayer to God, expressing submission to his will yet declaring the patient's desire to die? Such acceptance and empathy on your part will do far more for her than any negative, reactive, judgmental alternatives.

One *final* and important factor for the visitor to remember is that many more people are caught up in the dying process than the dying patient herself. Relatives of the patient and, to some degree, hospital staff share the experience. They too go through the emotional phases of dying, in some instances even more strongly than the patient. (We will look at these others in the next chapter. For now it is enough to be aware that they are part of the total picture, and will no doubt come into the orbit of your ministry to the dying.)

It is important in this ministry to realize that you may not be able to visit intensely for very long. Don't feel discouraged. Even for a professional, about three hours a day would be the maximum one could expect to work with the dying. The lay pastoral visitor should always feel that he can refer a patient to the minister if he's getting in deeper than he can manage. He needn't feel that he's abandoning the patient, but simply letting the pastor handle the "heavy" ministering. However, I'd encourage lay visitors to minister themselves as much as they can. Clergy have no monopoly in love and understanding, or in the skills of creative listening.

Have you thought how all this might apply to a dying child? Would it be harder to minister to a child? At first it may seem more than you could bear. But after you have dealt with your own feelings and can begin to look for what the child needs, it can be the most rewarding ministry of all. Nina Herrman writes about it in *Go Out With Joy*. I encourage you to read this book. Much can be done also for the parents of the child, and this too helps the child.

11

Ministry To Those Who Mourn

What do you do if you are present with relatives at the bedside when the patient draws her last breath? There's no stock answer to this question. But certainly the survivors have needs. Touching a shoulder or clasping a hand in silence may convey more support than many words. Sometimes it seems right to make some act of acknowledgement to God, some act of faith. Those who are accustomed to saying the Apostle's Creed might find it supportive to recite it together, ending as it does with the words, "I believe in. . . the communion of saints, the forgiveness of sins, the resurrection of the body, and the life everlasting." A brief prayer of thanks for the life of the deceased and the fellowship enjoyed with her in the past, together with a word commending her into God's hands, is usually appropriate and much appreciated.

How should you pray if you are uncertain about the faith of the deceased? We can never be dogmatic about a person's relationship with God. Only God himself knows that. We simply do not have absolute certainty. The bereaved are in no shape for religious debate at this point. They need your care. They need to feel the love of God through you. So if you pray with them, express thanks for things in the life of the deceased that you can be genuinely thankful for, recall gratefully before God the gracious atoning work of his Son, and relinquish the one who has died to his keeping and his mercy. Remember that at the time of the loved one's death, the relatives are in a state of shock. Their emotions, though possibly under control, are high. They are not at the moment in an intellectual "space." So do not try to teach them. Love and support them with thoughtful actions, with touch, with your presence, with your simple prayer. But be discreet. Do not dominate. Let them feel the love of God flowing from you. There is every possibility that they will want more attention later, and you or someone else can minister to them then.

The death will affect you too. You will definitely need to talk to someone. I hope you find a creative listener at such a time. His or her ministry can be an affirmation and a strength. If you belong to a lay pastoral visitors team, you can minister to one another. Remember: "No man is an island. . . any man's death diminishes me, because I am involved in mankind; and therefore never send to know for whom the bell tolls; it tolls for thee" (*Devotions XVII* — John Donne).

Immediate Practical Concerns

The relatives, soon after their loved one's demise, may express anxiety about what to do next. "What do we do with the body?" asks one. Another wonders, "How do I go about arranging the funeral?" The question often arises whether to permit the hospital to perform an autopsy. Your ministry at this time needs to be both supportive and practical. Here is some factual information which people may need, suggestions that can reduce some of the panic that results from not knowing what to do.

1 They will need to select a funeral director within the next twelve or fourteen hours. It can be one near their home or one their friends have mentioned. If the bereaved haven't a clue whom to approach, you might suggest the names of two or three funeral directors. This way you will not seem to be drumming up business for any one. If they do ask you which one you would choose, just give them a direct, non-persuasive answer.

2 Assure them that the details of picking up the body from the hospital, finding a burial plot, and so on, will be arranged with their approval by the funeral director. It is his job to guide people through all the practical matters of funeral arrangements.

3 If they have a minister whom they would like to conduct the funeral service, advise them to inform him immediately. If they do not have one, assure them that funeral directors are in touch with many retired clergy and other pastors who are glad to help out at such a time of need. There is no need to talk about fees here; the funeral director will ask the relatives what sort of honorarium they'd like to give the minister, and will advise them how to do it.

4 There is no need for the bereaved to linger in the hospital after the death. Once they have obtained all the information they need, you can check with the nurse to see whether anything remains to be done. She may then give them a bag containing the patient's valuables such as watch, wallet, and other personal belongings from the room. She may call the doctor who could possibly request permission to do an autopsy. When all this is done, they can

go home and contact the funeral director. Of course if the death occurs in the middle of the night, they may have to wait until morning to call him.

5 At some time during your conversation, you might suggest that they be ready to give the funeral director their answers to the following questions.

Do they want an ornate or simple coffin?

Do they want the body embalmed so that the coffin can be open, perhaps for several days, in the funeral home where visitors can come to pay their respects?

Do they wish no embalming, with the funeral the next day or very soon thereafter?

Do they want an open or a closed coffin?

Do they wish a burial or cremation, and if cremation, do they want to keep the ashes or have them buried in a marked or unmarked grave?

Do they want an announcement of the death and time of funeral put in the newspaper?

In order for a regular pastoral visitor to know about all this, he should, if he has the time, go to a funeral home, ask all sorts of questions, and satisfy himself regarding the various possibilities and the costs of different services offered. Then he'll be forearmed for any enquiry that anxious relatives may make.

6 Suppose the doctor asks for an autopsy. He may not feel able comfortably to explain why. You can perhaps help a little here. Autopsies serve to confirm or correct diagnoses that were made and treatments that were given, or may provide evidence of previously unknown factors. Their purpose is broadly educational. But they cannot be done without written permission from the next of kin. No pressure should be allowed to influence the bereaved's decision, and in no way should the refusal of an autopsy be reacted to judgmentally. The bereaved, incidentally, have a right to know the results of the autopsy. Only the doctor can give them this information. So if they want to know, they should ask him.

In the moments of shock that so often accompany death — no matter how long it has been expected — straightforward, non-pressure information that answers the question "What do I do now?" is a most useful and comforting service to offer to the immediately bereaved.

Normal Grief

Christians as well as others may be expected to grieve when a loved one dies. One of the saddest mistakes a Christian can make is to feel that expressions of sorrow or grief are evidence of loss of faith or of separation from the strengthening resources of the Holy Spirit. Quite the opposite is true. No Christian need submit to the stoicism of convention, or spiritual pride. There is a time to mourn as well as a time to dance (Eccles. 3:4). Jesus expressed grief at the grave of Lazarus his friend (John 11:33–36). He taught his disciples that they who mourn are blessed. He urged us not only to laugh with them that laugh, but to weep with them that weep (Matt. 11:17, see also Rom. 12:15). It's perfectly normal for Christians to grieve, though their grief has a difference because it is a grief with hope (I Thess. 4:13–14).

How do you go about ministering to people stricken with grief? First of all, you should arm yourself with some understanding of the normal grief process. Though each student of this universal human experience describes it differently, there are common elements. My own way of setting it down is just one among many. It is important to get the feel of what is happening to a person going through *normal grief*. It is necessary also to look at some aspects of *abnormal grief*, so that you will be able to recognize whether your friend or client is doing her normal and necessary "grief work" or whether she's showing signs of an unhealthy mental and emotional state.

Before we examine the usual phases of grief work (outlined below), we should take note two very common phenomena. The *first* is called *preparatory grief*. This occurs in advance of the loved one's death. Some people experience disturbing emotional ambivalence while a loved one is dying. A grieving widow may be alarmed to find herself becoming angry at her *deceased* spouse ("How could he leave me at a time like this? Doesn't he know how much I need him? Why didn't he go to the doctor when I first urged him? — and so on). But the wife of a *living* husband, whose death she awaits with dread, may experience the same reaction, even though she dearly loves him. There can be anger that he's taking too long to do what has to be done. At the same time there's deep yearning for continuance of the old relationship, and perhaps panic in the face of the inevitable loss.

The *second* phenomenon is the *grief that follows any loss* sustained by a person. The death of a spouse, a child, or any very dear one causes the deepest grief. The loss of a limb through amputation, loss of a job, a home or homeland can result in grief. Good grief work with regard to any loss can help a person grow. Left undone it can cause emotional or psychological harm that may actually lead to physical illness. Granger Westberg suggests that a surprisingly large number of sicknesses have some sort of loss and bad grief at their root. This means that most of the sick people you visit probably have some kind of problem with loss. Knowing this will help you to understand them.

I have divided the normal grieving experience into seven phases, not all of equal duration. These emotions and reactions come over the bereaved person in waves. For a while she may seem to be coping well with life; then a wave of denial, depression, loneliness, or guilt will overcome her. She'll seem to be fine again for awhile, then experience another wave. Here are the seven phases with some suggestions about ways of ministering. They can be remembered as the seven R's.

1 *Reeling*. When the loved one dies, no matter how long the family has expected it or how well thay are prepared, there is a period of shock. It's happened! A minute ago he was breathing. Now he's dead! There's a feeling of unreality. The most commonly heard words at this time are: "I can't believe it's really happened!" People feel numb. Their emotions haven't come into play yet. When a workman accidentally cuts off his finger, there is no pain for a few moments, and he stares at his hand in disbelief. But the reaction of anesthesia lasts only seconds. After that, pain!

So it is with the suddenly bereaved. You cannot change this feeling. As friend and pastoral visitor you have to accept it. The support of your presence will help the grieving person more than anything else at this time. (Some of the suggestions at the beginning of this chapter concerning what to do or what to say if you're there at the moment of death may prove useful.)

2 *Rejection*. This is just another word for denial. (You'll notice as we go through these stages how many of them correspond to the stages a dying person goes through. That is because the dying person, too, is grieving — about the separations and the losses that are to come. In a sense, as far as human emotions and reactions are concerned, the phases of dying and the phases of grieving could come under one heading: *reactions to loss.*)

The bereaved ones tend to deny the reality of their loved one's death. "It's not true!" they say. "It can't be! Look! Isn't he still breathing?" Their emotions cannot comprehend the facts that their intellects know are true. I have seen people actually shake the dead body, slap the face, yell into the ear in an effort to revive the dead person. The more stoic types will keep this all inside, but the inner conflict of feelings versus reality is there just the same. Even after the body has been taken to the funeral parlor, there's a feeling that he really can't be dead. And the illusion may linger for days. This period of denial seems to be a necessary psychological defence mechanism, unconsciously brought into play to buffer the shock of the loss.

Denial may be necessary in another way too, as with a child who screamed at the corpse, "Come back Daddy, come back." And at God, too: "You've got to send him back. You've got to, you've got to!" All this may be terribly distressing to the bystanders, and naturally they'll be concerned lest the child (or adult) stay in this phase too long. But later on it may be a great satisfaction to the bereft child to know that he tried his hardest to get his daddy back. He tried and failed. If he hadn't tried, he might feel guilty for having given up too easily.

3 *Release.* Now the reality of the death sinks in. He really is gone. There's no more numbness. No more rejecting the facts. The feeling of loss takes over and the crying may begin. The person may get to this stage very quickly, within minutes. Or it may take days. If it takes much longer than that, begin to think of special help — perhaps from the minister. It is not normal to reject reality for very long.

But what of the "normal" griever? What can you do with a weeping mourner? You can show by your acceptance that it's OK to cry. Remember how Jesus wept for Lazarus. You can, if you're so moved, genuinely weep with the one who weeps. That can be a real blessing for her.

4 *Realization.* This is a long phase. It can start a day or two after the funeral, or perhaps a week or two after. It's a slow comprehension of the reality of the loss. Every little thing reminds the bereft widow of the deceased. There's only one place at breakfast now instead of two. Sometimes out of habit, she'll put out two coffee mugs, then realize with a pang that he's not there. Another wave of depression will overwhelm her. Even if she goes away for a vacation, she'll miss him. She's accustomed to saying, "Come look at this picture, dear." or "Isn't that a beautiful sunset!" She may start to say it. Or she may imagine hearing him say it. Going away doesn't solve any problems. It often adds to them, because not

having him to share the excitement just brings on more poignant realizations of the loss. It's a phase that has to be suffered; but it can be suffered well if there are understanding, accepting people around, like you.

You can reassure her that occasional illusions of having the deceased one there with her, her preoccupation with the one who has died, and recurrent distancing of herself from the people around her are quite natural, not signs of going crazy. She may even have an occasional hallucinatory vision of the departed. But if she recognizes the hallucination as incompatible with reality, then it is not a symptom of mental illness. It's normal deep grief. If a person having such hallucinations cannot be reassured by you or even by her minister, a psychologist can probably lay her fears to rest and reassure her that she's going through normal grief work.

As the days go by in this phase of realization, it is unfortunate that friends generally give up their frequent contacts with the bereaved, believing that she's now past the crisis and is "doing fine." As a matter of fact she probably needs them now more than ever. Two or three weeks after the funeral a period of real depression may begin. There will be much crying, secret or open. It can be emotional torture for the mourner to go to the regular services at the old church; so she may prefer the quiet early morning service, the prayer group, or services on TV. She feels unbearably lonely. You can't jolly her out of this, but you can help her carry on the functions of life as realistically as possible. It is a mistake, though, to indulge the person's tendency to wallow in self pity.

During this time, physical symptoms may appear. The body then is telling the person she must really do something more constructive about working out her grief. Always check the symptoms with a doctor, just in case there may be other factors involved.

Anger at God, anger at the doctor, anger at the deceased himself is normal. A person who knows the scriptures can help by showing how the psalmist (Psalm 77) or Job (in chapter 10, for example) spoke angry words to God. When angry feelings come, the worst thing is to pretend they are not real or to make the person feel guilty. On the contrary, acknowledge them; they are very human.

The person may feel guilty about other things. If she has been embezzling the deceased or was deliberately mean to him then she truly does need to acknowledge the reality of her guilt, confess it to God with repentance, and receive God's forgiveness through Christ. The pastoral visitor can gently lead a person through this painful process, giving assurance from God's word that the repentant sinner really is forgiven, accepted, and restored.

Some feelings of guilt have no foundation whatsoever in fact. A person can feel guilty just because she remains healthy and alive, whereas the loved one died. Such a person is becoming neurotic. She needs reassurance that this feeling is not based in fact. She can be helped to see things more clearly, and to realize that her guilt arises out of grief or emotional turmoil, not out of any specific sin connected with the death. The pastoral visitor can help the griever to accept the fact that unrealistic though her guilt feelings are, they are a normal experience and can be expected to pass. I do not mean that you have to argue the person into this acknowledgement. Allow her the right to her feelings and to the expression of them, but do not accept the false perspective which they imply.

Parents of children who die unaccountably from what is known as "sudden infant death syndrome" often feel excruciating mental pain and unbearable guilt because they were unable to prevent the death. They may berate themselves for not doing this or that, especially for not being in the child's immediate presence when the death happened, assuming that they could have prevented the death had they been there. They will undergo loss of sleep and appetite, inability to concentrate, unreasonable fears and anxieties over surviving children. Such symptoms can be expected to last perhaps a month. If they last longer, professional help is needed to deal with the debilitating emotion.

In all these aspects of grieving, it is a good thing to get the bereaved person to talk. Be a good, creative listener — back to the basic lesson! Often just by asking how it happened, you can help open the floodgates and enable the person to release the emotional pressure.

5 *Resistance.* This means resistance to change. Throughout the previous phases of grief, the bereaved is still oriented toward the past, toward what has happened to the loved one and to herself. There is a tendency to hang on and to salvage what one can. This too is normal, and the visitor must accept it. But an occasional hint about the future may help the bereaved to step out of this orientation. "What do you think you'll do about your summer holiday?" "Can I help you decide what to do with all his books?" The visitor should listen for cues indicating that the bereaved is

starting to think of the future and then gently encourage her in that direction. The mourner is at last regaining her grasp on reality!

6 *Reality*. Eventually the bereaved will come through to a balanced attitude toward reality. It may be a year before she gets this far. She'll feel, as well as know, that God is still there to help her through life, even without her dear one. She'll discover that the Lord has provided inner resources to deal with crises like this, and she'll begin to stir herself and use them. "I can't go on moping like this forever," she might say. "I've got to get out and do something."

She will begin to realize that she's not the only one who's ever suffered loss. There are people all around whose loved ones are dying. Now she can understand their hurt and support them. Some are even worse off than she's been. She can weep for them now, not just for herself.

She's even acquiring a new awareness and appreciation of the beauties and joys of life. She begins to count her blessings and to thank God again. You can help her in this. The pain of loss remains, but the sting of it is gone. The void is still there, but the raw edges are healed over. She begins to see that she's survived a personal tragedy and that, by the grace of God and with the support of true friends, she has really grown. Occasional waves of grief will continue to come over her, but they will become, more and more, waves of "sweet sorrow." She'll turn her thoughts and efforts to things that come to matter in a new way. She'll not exactly build a *new* life for herself, but reconstruct the life she knows already.

7 *Reconstruction*. She has the feeling now that life must go on. She *wants* it to go on. She's been through the valley of the shadow with God, emerged whole, and is ready to live. Friends can now encourage her desire to do new work, to engage in new activities both for fun and for helping and serving others. She'll seek out and find practical ways of using mental and physical energies. She may give herself wholeheartedly to some great cause such as care of the retarded, crippled children, hospital volunteer work, the cancer society, spiritual help for widows and widowers, or church work and evangelism. The old memories will always be there, but she'll learn to thank God for them and for the way she has grown from them. Loneliness will return at times, but she'll become adept at making realistic arrangements to deal with these episodes.

These, then, are the seven aspects or phases of normal grief work.

They do not always come in the above sequence, but they constitute a broad movement of normal grief that we can expect to happen: reeling, rejection, release, realization, resistance, reality, reconstruction. One psychiatrist, Dr M. O. Vincent of Homewood Sanitarium in Guelph, Ontario, groups these normal stages under three main headings: *first,* emancipating oneself from the one who has died, *second,* accepting and dealing with the reality of life without deceased, and *third,* building new relationships with people, in the process of which some of the personal needs once filled by the deceased will be satisfied in new ways. This is a simpler division, and one that I find very helpful in remembering the needs of a grieving person.

Grief in the Hospital Itself

A hospital visitor will probably encounter all of these stages. When ministering to the relatives of a person who is slowly dying, you may find them undergoing preparatory grief, possibly even beginning to reconstruct their life before the loved one is gone. Most often, however, it is when someone has just died that you'll be helping people who are reeling, rejecting or releasing their emotions. The nurse may be thoughtful enough to give you a room where you can sit with them as they talk out their denial, their sense of unreality, and as they weep. Toward the end of this time, practical information about funerals may be appropriate.

But this is not the last you'll see of grief in the hospital. Many people in medical and surgical wards are there because unresolved grief is making them sick. Accident-prone people in orthopedic wards may have got into difficulty through incompleted grief work. Many a person lying ill in bed has, in addition to his sickness, the burden of a loss to grieve. She needs your ministry for that just as much as she needs the surgery, the medicine, and the physiotherapy. Perhaps more. And we must not forget the nurses. They naturally become attached to patients who are there a long time. They too experience grief. They may not have time to receive much ministry from you, but your understanding of their plight will help them.

Grieving Children

Do not forget the children of the bereaved family. They need ministry too. We often suppose that a death does not affect them as much as it does the adults, but this is a big mistake. Their feelings may not show, but they are there and affect them deeply. Children have the added problem of not really understanding what death is.

They too have feelings of guilt. "If I'd been a really good girl, maybe this wouldn't have happened." If you're a good listener, they may confide in you their fears about ghosts, anger at God, and perplexity as to why God took grandma off to heaven. It does not normally help to shelter them from the experience of the funeral. Indeed, attending the funeral, with supportive loved ones around, can help them to acknowledge the reality of death, and can provide an "excuse" to express their emotions. It may also form the basis of a gratifying memory that "I did everything I was supposed to do, and grandma is probably happy about that."

One little girl, after talking with her minister, decided to go to her own mother's funeral. She confided that though it might be a shock, she knew Mummy was really with God, and she would rather suffer the shock than "miss something." "Death is not bad," she said, "It's just sad." After the funeral she remarked, "People should always go. It helps to keep you from being afraid to die." She was quite able to receive what the minister said to her: "It's God's world, and dying is part of it. I think it is all right to die. The Bible says 'whether I live or whether I die, I am the Lord's'."[11]

It is wrong to overprotect children, but it is not necessary to talk brutally or clinically about death. One little boy in hospital kept asking people what it was like to die. They gave all kinds of answers, and some advised him not to dwell on the subject. Then a good listener came along who was able openly to say she didn't really know, even though she had some ideas about it. But what did the little fellow think? He replied what all along he was really wanting to say, "I think it's like going to sleep on a train in one place, and when you wake up you're somewhere else." I heard Dr Kubler-Ross tell that story.

A lay hospital visitor should know what good grief is, and be able to minister to anyone, patient or relative, in whatever phase of grieving he finds him or her. Such knowledge will nurture an ever deepening understanding of how loss hurts people, and of ways in which Christ's servants can minister to those hurts.

12

Ministry To The Elderly

Why devote a special chapter to visiting the elderly in hospital? There are several good reasons. First of all, we are bound to find ourselves visiting more people over sixty-five as the years go by. The proportion of senior citizens in our society will reach the twenty-percent mark by the year two thousand, and some pockets of the continent have a higher percentage of elderly even now. Secondly, people in this age bracket need hospitalization approximately three times as often as those under sixty-five. There are also increasing numbers of elderly people in senior citizens' homes and in nursing homes. Hundreds live alone in the community, and a fair number still stay in families with spouse, brother or sister, or children. If we learn how to minister to the aged so that we can help others learn from us, we ourselves will probably benefit from the others' ministries when we reach old age ourselves.

For Christians there is a more fundamental obligation to visit the elderly. Honoring the old person and showing him or her the deepest respect is a way of honoring God himself (Lev. 19:32). The faithful are required to regard the "hoary head" as a crown of glory (Prov. 16:31). This means that first names, and such presumptuously intimate words of address as "dearie," should be avoided. Instead give full respect by using surnames with Miss, Mrs or Mr. Of course, if a person asks you to use his first name, go ahead.

A further motivation for the Christian's special concern for the care of the elderly is found in the writings of Saint Paul. Paul says that anyone who does not care for his own, especially those of his own household, is failing his duty and is worse than an infidel (1 Tim. 5:8). The context of this passage seems to imply that we owe a responsibility to the elderly of quite a wide circle, not immediate family members alone. I think Paul refers also to the elderly of the congregation, our older brothers and sisters in Christ. In Paul's day that particularly meant widows.

We need those elders. They have talents, gifts, and wisdom of experience that younger ones sorely lack. Their physical handicaps and inevitable slowing down in no way detract from the value of their human potential. Not only do the elderly have resources, they also have leisure to make use of them, if only we avoid blocking their opportunities. Christian stewardship requires that we let none of these treasures go to waste. Besides, our elders have common human needs which in Christian love we are obligated to meet. They continue to need from others the same love and sense of worth, the same assurance of meaning in their lives, the same acceptance and forgiveness as they did when they were young. They need some stimulation and excitement too, as we all do.

It would be very easy to expand our concern for the elderly into community attitudes and responsibilities to the elderly, an area where much active Christian work needs constantly to be done. We could enlarge on the special opportunities for churches to serve the elderly, especially those who, because of reduced mobility, can't easily swell the attendance at morning worship. These same persons are often unable to give money. But should we let that decrease the esteem in which we hold them? Surely not. Sometimes, because of depression and loneliness, the elderly seem to withdraw into their own little worlds and get forgotten. That is very sad. In hospital I meet older people who have become lost to their clergy and congregations because no one made the effort to keep in touch. People like these need Christian visitors more than anyone else.

There is much more to be said about the way our churches treat their elderly people. (I refer my readers to some of the books in the bibliography.) Suffice it to emphasize that a deliberate effort must be made to keep older Christians involved in the fellowship of our congregations. Without this conscious effort and attention they will all too easily fall by the wayside in the headlong scramble of activities planned and run by the young. We have an obligation to help our elderly feel genuinely valued as church members. Without them we ourselves are incomplete.

Myths of Old Age

Let us consider the practicalities of visiting the elderly, especially in hospital. How exactly are we to go about it? That question is impossible to answer without looking at some of the myths commonly associated with old age.

  1 The elderly are much alike. Answer: Differences among the
    elderly are more pronounced than among people of other age

groups. They have had many more years than most of us to develop along individual lines. The longer people live, the more they become differentiated in personality, life-style, motivation, interests, character. Through the teens, early marriage years, and middle age the life-routes chosen and the life-goals followed present a growing picture of infinitely varied color, purpose, and value.

The interests and differences of people sixty-five and over become even more varied yet. Their rates of aging vary immensely. Their health histories cannot be lumped indiscriminately together. There is no such person as "your average senior citizen." How hopeless a task therefore to answer the question, "How should we visit old people?" — even the ones that are in hospital. The only uniformity in our hospitalized elders is that most of them are in beds. The first part of the answer to our question about how to visit the aged, then, is really another question: "Which particular aged person do you have in mind?" Let us dismiss forever the myth that they're all alike.

2 "You can't teach an old dog new tricks." Answer: seniors are not just animals, and you *can* teach if you know how.

3 "Ability to learn and grow intellectually decreases with age." Answer: the *ability* decreases only minimally, even though the *speed* of learning may become less. This deficit is amply outbalanced by a generally steadier application to learning willingly undertaken.

4 "You can't change human nature." Answer: *we* can't change *them* or anyone else, but *they* can change *themselves* with God's help. God created mankind to grow mentally, morally, and spiritually, as well as in other ways.

5 "Old persons lose interest in their sexuality." Answer: they are still men and still women; they know it and are glad of it. While their interest in each other mellows and matures, interest in persons of the opposite sex nevertheless remains and adds worth to earthly existence and relationships.

6 "Old age changes the personality." The truth is that, barring a dramatic religious conversion, one's personal development generally carries on in the same direction that it has taken during earlier years.

7 "The aged cannot adapt to changes or cope with pressures." Answer: Everyone to his own taste. If some older people prefer

Lawrence Welk to the Rolling Stones, who's to say they're wrong? If they like gospel hymns or traditional liturgies, it's their choice. Many of the aged cope better than most young people. Humans have more problems to deal with in the last twenty years of their average seventy-two years than they ever had in their youth. Most of them adapt extremely competently, probably due to their maturity.

8 "Old people become inactive and just give up on life." Answer: nothing could be further from the truth. Many are more creative and active in their senior years than they had been previously, despite diseases and handicaps, and the restraints that society inflicts on them.

9 The greatest myth of all is *the myth of senility.* Hospital visitors need to be acutely aware of this. There actually is no such disease as senility. It is merely a name given to a combination of conditions which afflict the elderly. You don't catch senility. It is not inevitable in old people. Senility is a *label* that has become a *libel.* What we call senility can be a combination of (a) pathology of the brain, (b) general poor health, (c) decreasing environmental stimuli, especially the stimuli of other people, and (d) the personality which the individual has developed over the years.

   The condition of senility can be affected and even changed by alterations in any of these factors, and we have the power to make some of the changes. We cannot, of course, invade the personality and change that by ourselves. But we can change the environment. We can change the amount and kind of stimulation provided by people. Brain pathology and bodily diseases we have to leave to the doctors, though our prayers can make a difference. Younger people become afflicted by many of these same threats to health, and we never give up on them. Should we give up on the older ones just because they are soon going to die?

10 It is a pathetic myth that care of the aged is easier than care of the younger. We are beginning at last to recognize that nurses, social workers, and pastoral visitors who choose geriatric care require not fewer skills but many more. They need special understanding of the needs and capabilities of the elderly. Why does the myth persist among us that it doesn't take much intelligence to care for old people? It doesn't take much skill to care for young mothers or crippled athletes either, if you ignore them!

It is our attitude to such myths that will be the greatest contributing factor in our style of ministry to the aged. Seniors you visit in hospital are far from dull people. Unfortunately, some seniors hear these myths so often that, despite their positive self-image, the pressure and insistence of our prejudices set up doubts in their own minds. They, as well as we, need to be convinced that the myths are false. The false assumptions we've been looking at here constitute the latest ugly "ism" of our times, a pathetic rival for racism and sexism. Maggie Kuhn calls it *agism*.

Old people need support and encouragement to escape the snares of agism and to stay involved in life as much as they can. It is our privilege to help them use their talents and gifts in new and imaginative ways, to benefit both others and themselves. Gerontologists project that a human's fullest intellectual potential is seldom reached before the age of sixty or seventy! Seniors need to learn how to fight back, to resist society's constant brainwashing. Like most of us they need the ability to be self-starters despite the non-co-operation they so often encounter from others. One place we can begin to show real appreciation of old people is when they're sick, in hospital.

Some Common Needs Of The Aged

How can we know what kind of ministry our particular elderly patient needs? Most of us have no personal experience of being old. Only a bare inkling of the old person's feelings and needs is possible to us, based on what we've been taught by books, lectures, and old people themselves. A lively eighty-year old pastoral visitor from an Ontario church told me that she is the best pastoral visitor for the elderly in her community because she knows what it's like to be old. Because of our inexperience, therefore, we are forced to *be learners as well as ministers*. We really have to be creative listeners!

The following are some guidelines from my own thirty years of pastoral work.

Though every aged person is unique, we do know in advance some of the basic general needs of all the elderly. We should be ready to minister to these and to become increasingly aware of individual human needs earlier in the book (chapter 2): love, worth, meaning, forgiveness, acceptance, stimulation, God. The way you minister to forgiveness, acceptance, stimulation, God. The way you minister to these needs begins in your attitude, in your love for people born out of your experience of God's love and forgiveness to you.

People of all ages experience other needs, but some of these are often felt more keenly by people in old age. For one thing, elders experience *more losses* than most of us: physical losses such as failing eyesight and hearing, loss of mobility and facility in the use of limbs, loss of taste sensation, loss of strength, energy, and health. Our elders gradually lose their friends and relatives through death. Most painful is the loss of a spouse. Senior citizens, because of mandatory retirement, also lose their place in the workforce. Almost universally there is loss of income after the age of sixty-five.

Because of the many losses they have to suffer, seniors can feel very lonely. Pastoral visitors can assume without threat of contradiction that a great many of our elders are engaged in a constant battle against the depression of loneliness and rejection, both when they're well and when they're ill. Could it be that some become ill because that is the only way they can receive a little attention and love from other people? Many undoubtedly have a lurking fear that their days may end in isolation and rebuff. Consider your own feelings regarding the five, ten, twenty, or perhaps thirty years of old age that you may experience. The concern is not far from all of us.

Some old people, especially in institutions, become very irascible. They perhaps are persons who throughout life have not been accustomed to taking a back seat. Some of them may have been chronic complainers all their lives. Experience has shown, however, that often this behaviour is the elder's way of fighting apparent dismissal from the human race. It is their angry protest at our putting them on the shelf. The "difficult" resident of a nursing home may be the one who is most alert to what's going on. Her complaining may actually be a good sign, an indication that she's aware of what's happening, and is insisting on some rights and a degree of participation in decisions concerning her welfare. She may indeed be demanding more out of life than days spent in a wheelchair, sitting with a row of similarly handicapped people. We need to use our imaginations to discover what such difficult people are trying to say to us. They definitely need our attention, and the stimulation of relating to us. We ought to use our sense of humor for them (at our own expense, of course, not theirs). Perhaps with a more human touch we can help them break out of their solitary confinement.

Would it not be a shame to force silence and unquestioning compliance on such people? We could be tempted to do just that for our own convenience, so impatient are we to get on with our own agendas for them. What of their own right to choose, to make decisions for themselves, to have a voice in what happens to them? Loss of the right to participate in decisions about themselves is one of the most infuriating things that some seniors are forced to suffer. Loneliness and dependence: hard pills to swallow! But much of the time the aged really need not have to endure them. The company and ministry of loving and practical friends can help immensely in overcoming these afflictions.

The threat of a lonely, empty, and meaningless existence, however, cannot be overcome merely by environmental changes such as stronger stimuli and the presence of friends. Old people must be encouraged to build up their own inner resources of faith, courage, and determination in order themselves to slay the dragon of isolation. Certainly trust in God opens up resources that nothing else can. We can build people up in that trust, not just by words, as Saint James says (James 2:14–16), but by deeds. Congregations can arrange to involve the elderly in church life, to keep in constant touch with them, and to accept the contributions that they can make. Pastoral visitors may have to lead the church in intelligent efforts and imaginative means to help the elderly stay in circulation.

The elder's losses, as they pile up, may trigger changes both mental and physical that adversely affect their health. Loss of memory can become a source of worry and anxiety. The words, "I'm afraid I'm losing my mind," express a genuine dread of many seniors. They need reassurance and encouragement not to accept the condition as an inevitable part of growing old. A trip to the doctor may help to reassure them and to make possible some kind of treatment that could remedy loss of the memory.

Other needs of the aged can be listed more briefly. Many in hospital fear being idle and useless more than they fear death. Others may have neurotic pre-occupations with bodily symptoms such as constipation or headaches. But are such fears confined only to the aged? Surely not! So let's not riducule their concern. It is an embarrassment, too, for an old man to have to be bathed, helped on to the toilet or bedpan, and fed like a baby by a young nurse who could be his grand-daughter. Many such distressing things have to be done to the patient for health's sake. Another humiliation is a urine bag attached to a catheter tube which drains the patient's bladder. It has to go everywhere he or she goes. Not everyone can use the embarrassing catheter. Incontinence can then be mortifying for a patient, as can occasional accidents of defecation. Half-hour changes of urine-soaked sheets may be necessary. Don't add to the patient's mortification by showing your embarrassment or by talking about this with a nurse or friend where the patient can hear. You may experience bad smells from a patient's rectal drainage or leaky colostomy. Don't let these external things, these apparent indignities, blind you to the person behind them, the person who so much needs your love, acceptance, and care.

The patient may be confused as to time, where she is, what's happened to her. Dreams, hallucinations, and reality may merge in her perception, due to medication or brain damage. This can be very hard on loved ones. Overanxious or emotionally unsettled relatives may actually need more ministry from you than the patient herself.

The patient tied to her chair may be there because otherwise she might harm herself. There may not be enough staff available to watch her every second. Not an ideal situation by any standards! But often there's little else that can be done. This need not prevent you from trying to find ways of keeping old people out of such a "prison." Depending on personality, the reactions of patients to their confined situations may be passivity and withdrawal, quarrelsomeness, persistent demands, hysterical dependence, deep depression, or anxiety. If you feel you have to succeed in cheering up all these people and in changing everyone's life, you yourself will experience constant failure and depression. On the other hand, if you can love them and try to do what you can, you'll receive rewards you never hoped for.

It helps to remember that any ministry, to be effective, has to be *received*. The patient too has an important part to play. We for our part can learn to give help in as acceptable form as possible. We can train ourselves to look and listen for the kind of help the patient is reaching out for. Yet, if all we can do is just be present and attentive, then we must offer that as our reasonable service.

What are some interests that the elderly have? Again we remind ourselves that individual elders are unique. Yet those who are religious, who all their lives have believed in God and in the life to come, share in common a much deeper interest in that life now that their time of departure draws near.

For religious people earthly interests are seen more and more in the radiant light of the greater life to come. Many want desperately to talk about that life. They wonder what heaven will be like. There's wistful, forward-looking uncertainty about the mystery of eternal life. The certainty of God's love, his forgiveness, his promises, and scriptural allusions to the quality of that future life capture their imaginations. Assurances from the scriptures about these things and reminders of them in favourite hymns mean much to such devout and expectant elders. If a person wants to talk about dying, by all means let her. She may say, "I'm ready to go, but I'm certainly not anxious for it to happen too soon," or "I can hardly wait to go and join Harry," or somewhat wistfully, "I know I'll have to go soon, and I wonder if God has a place for me there." If you're a creative listener, she may venture to disclose any number of such feelings.

I've mentioned that one of the commonest fears older people have about dying is being abandoned by everyone. Perhaps they sense our discomfort with the fact of death or the very process of dying — the deterioration of their faculties, the indignities they suffer. The sick old person can sense that people are deserting her. She may see it happening to her peers and is afraid lest it happen to her too. The patient may think of suicide, and mention it to her listening lay visitor. She may agitate for someone to "pull the plug" on life-support systems. Acknowledge and accept the feelings. Don't pretend that she doesn't have such thoughts, and don't scold her for them. Try to be aware also when similar thoughts occur in your own mind. Don't tell the patient all about them, but do let your own experience help you understand her predicament.

Be ready for the senior who has no viable church connection but has a deep faith, and may pray, read the Bible, or watch services on TV. She's like a branch of the vine connected to it by a long, weak stem. Do what you can to restore the neglected connections, without smothering her with guilty love. Many a time the fault for her estrangement from the church lies mainly with a congregation that has simply passed her by and lost touch. There are old people who are agnostics or atheists, and there are people who have become quite soured on religion. The last thing they need is a Bible-thumper to impose himself on them. Genuine caring, on the other hand, is hard to resist.

Let us be aware of some of the things we *cannot* do for the elderly patient. Of course we can't prescribe medicine or perform therapy. We may be aware that disorientation (often mistakenly called senility) can be caused by low blood pressure, by blood settling in the abdomen from long periods of sitting, by decrease in body potassium as a result of excessive use of laxatives. These and other difficulties can be ministered to only by the doctor and his staff. Some of a patient's confusion is avoidable, if only busy nurses, orderlies, and volunteers would understand that the old patient needs to have procedures explained to her. These remarks apply to hospital staff, I realize. But the visitor, though he cannot usually tell the doctor or orderly what to do, can reassure the patient that so many things happening at once could confound anybody. You could admit that you'd be the same way in the midst of so many changes and unknowns. If the nurse or doctor has explained things to you, you might help, with his permission, by explaining to the patient. We should exert what little influence we may have to ensure that we do not confuse patients by rushing them about as if they were robots on an assembly line, impersonal objects, apparently not wanted or cared for.

We can try to help patients realize their important position in the healing process. They have the final say, the final consent. Patients do not perceive themselves as mere victims of the treatments of a half-dozen professionals. One very positive thing to remember about older people is their way of compensating for physical losses, even such losses as nerve cells. You may be able to give additional help in this regard. Stronger stimuli of color, action, and sound can compensate for failing vision and hearing. Poor eyesight can be helped by brighter light. Poor hearing can be dealt with by your using a lower but louder tone of voice. It's the higher frequencies of sound and voice that are hardest for the elderly to hear. It is important for you to speak very distinctly too.

Sometimes you'll run across a patient who's full of self-pity, unwilling to work at living. If you've earned this person's friendship and affection, you may be able to rouse her to increased vitality by a sharp challenge or rebuke (not a condemnation). One volunteer I know, who herself is over eighty, has helped many of her peers by such firm but caring confrontations.

Goals in Visiting the Elderly

What should our goals be in visiting the elderly patient? A nurse gives what I believe is the best answer: medically to treat for a cure and, if that is not possible, to alleviate suffering and help the patient cope with his incapacities.[12] How, you may ask, are these goals and ministries different from the ones we have for younger patients? No different at all, really. We do the elderly a distinct disservice by regarding them as greatly different from people of other age groups. When we do this we stereotype them, pigeonhole them, fence them in with iron-clad attitudes. This is exactly what they do not need. They're still part of our life and we part of theirs. We and they have many things to say to each other. They are aging, but so are we.

Be ready to join in *significant conversation* with them. This is probably the most helpful ministry that you as a visitor can offer to an elderly person. Too many people refuse to allow the elderly into their minds and lives in serious, as contrasted with jolly and superficial, conversation. Reminiscing can be very helpful for an older person. It is one way she can affirm that she was not always on the fringes of life's activities, that she has experienced and accomplished some really important things during her time in this world. To reminisce one needs an attentive listener.

The elderly need people who have *faith in them* and in what they can do, people who know that moods and motivations do change. The way a person is on one day is not necessarily the way she'll be the next. People have been known to emerge from so-called senility; and often the main factor in their emergence has been the stimulating company of caring people over a period of time.

For *practical helps* it is useful for the visitor to know, or at least to have access to, information about community services for the elderly: day-care programs, home nursing care, public health services, financial counseling, courses, church groups, and others who can provide rides for shopping and arrange parish get-togethers for wheelchair patients when they go home.

What of patients who do not respond to anything you try to do? There are those who absolutely cannot respond. How can you have a successful ministry with them? Well, they are still God's valued children. Show that you *value them* in the best way you can. You're there not to achieve success for yourself but to minister to the patient's need. There's much evidence to show that people who do not or cannot respond to your attempts at ministry are nevertheless somehow aware of your presence and the attitude that you bring to the bedside. Speak to them, read to them, pray for them, even if they're comatose. God accepts the ministry as done to his Son, and he hears and uses your prayer.

When visiting an elderly patient whose nervous system cannot cope with too much input all at once, *go alone*. If you do have to take a second visitor with you, don't both talk at once. Decide ahead of time who will do the talking. The other can pray silently, listen, and help afterwards in evaluating your approach. Some people can give cues and signals to you even though they can't talk; so be imaginative in your reception of these. If there are two of you visiting, the observer may be of some help in interpreting cues both during and after the visit.

If a patient seems to want a walk or a wheelchair ride outside or around the halls, be sure to check first with the nurse. Be prepared to read things or to write letters, cards, or notes for patients who cannot do it themselves. Helping with a meal if the nurse approves, is OK *provided* your patient is not embarrassed to be fed or to eat in front of you. Many elderly who have alert minds but inadequate coordination may slop their food or drool. So don't insist on helping where you're really not wanted. You'll learn new things every day that will help you be sensitive to the patient's real need, and to keep in check your own need to be of assistance.

The Visitor's Own Needs

Many of the problems of the elderly are not essentially theirs at all, but ours in not accepting them and relating to them as they are. Part of our ministry therefore is regularly to examine ourselves, so that we'll not burden the patients with our inadequacies. Be conscious of the possibility that any unresolved problems about or relationships with your own parents, feelings that you have not yet learned to manage, may make it hard for you to relate openly and realistically with a person who is the same age as your parent. If you have not yet been able to cut the apron-strings or struggle out from under the hurts and resentments of parental domination, you may unconsciously relate in a guarded or even belligerent way to other elders. You could too easily close them out of your inner life. It works the other way too. Guilt-feelings about mean ways in which you treated your own parents may cause you to overcompensate with older patients by smothering kindness and protectiveness.

Another problem may be your attitude toward your approaching old age and your own death. If you have worked through these, you'll be more free to perceive and minister to the patient's needs when you're with her. The best preparation for visiting anyone is to find integrity and peace with God and with your fellow-man. Whatever you do for your own improvement will have, as an inevitable spin-off, advantages for whoever else you happen to meet.

13

How To Visit On The Psychiatric Ward

Some pastoral visitors are nervous about visiting anyone on the psychiatric ward of the general hospital. The same applies to many clergy. Perhaps this is good in a way. It may prevent their barging in and thoughtlessly saying and doing things that are unhelpful. It may increase sensitivity, and that is good. I should hope it would not lead to overcompensation with a false bravado and pseudo *savoire faire* that could really gum things up. If you're a bit nervous, just accept yourself as such and don't pretend to be otherwise. That's safe ground on which to start. It's OK to be cautious in a new venture like this, if it is out of concern for the patient. As soon as you learn the truth about psychiatric wards, you'll lose some of that anxiety while retaining your openness to the feelings of others and your concern to assist the therapy.

Psychiatric patients, generally speaking, are like you and me. They have troubles, just as we do. They get depressed, over-elated, fearful; they have irrational terrors, deceive themselves, have delusions of grandeur. But psychiatric patients experience these troubles with far greater intensity than most of us — at least to a degree they cannot bear without help. By far the most patients one meets in psychiatry seem to be depressed in some way or another. You'll find some alcoholics too. Alcoholism is today's number one mental health problem, according to Dr Howard Clinebell. Quite a few patients are withdrawn, extremely so. Others are manic, exceedingly "hyper," excitable, and over-stimulated.

But they are all people. You do not need to be afraid of them or even afraid of hurting them, so long as you go to them with sensitivity and common sense. They have the same human needs that we've seen before. They need to be loved, accepted, cared for. They need meaning in their lives. Just by going to pay a visit you show your friend that you care. Don't think that every word you say during the visit has to be censored before you utter it. Show that you care by *constantly* visiting. Let it not be a one-time gesture.

Psychiatric patients stay in hospital longer than most others, except chronic and terminally ill patients. Whereas the average stay in surgery may be eight or ten days, the average stay in psychiatry is approximately twenty. Some stay for two months, even longer where this is allowed.

Will you be welcomed by the psychiatric staff on the ward? You definitely will. They want the patients to socialize, to meet people, to overcome their fear of others, to learn to cope with living in the real world of persons. Of course you must observe the visiting hours. Clergy sometimes are able to visit in psychiatry outside of visiting hours. The main thing is to check with the nurse that it's convenient and not disruptive of any rest time, therapy schedule, group session, or whatever. None of these things are done during visiting hours.

You would be well advised to visit only your own friends or people from your congregation whom your pastor asks you to visit. Let that be a basic rule of thumb, though it is possible to stretch it a little here and there, where appropriate. Do *not* go to the psychiatric floor to "cruise around" looking for people to meet and minister to. There are visitors who like to do just that, and they must be discouraged. It is an invasion of the privacy of patients and an intrusion into the structured life of the ward which is under the care and supervision of the staff. Floating do-gooders are a menace.

If you have flowers or a gift to bring, be sure to ask for permission at the nursing station. You never know whether there may be a reason to keep such things from a patient, at least for a time.

How should you behave during the visit? Here are a few hints. First of all, make it a rule always to check in at the nursing station; say who you are and whom you want to visit. Then ask if there is anything you should be aware of or be careful about. This gesture of co-operation will be much appreciated. After the first time or two, you may only need to wave as you go by. The staff will get to know you fairly quickly.

When you're with the patient, have an ordinary conversation. Be a good listener, but don't try to counsel or be an amateur psychologist. It may be a great temptation for you to do so, but resist if for the time being.

Provide good companionship and act naturally as a friend. Christian patients sometimes feel guilty about being admitted to the psychiatric ward. Do avoid even a hint of judgmental behaviour or speech. Do not get into arguments or wax persuasive. If a patient is able to discuss things of interest, that would seem to be all right so long as you don't become aggressive or domineering. When in doubt, you can always check with the nurse.

The essence of your ministry is the giving of yourself as a caring visitor. Give your presence and your conversation. Pray before you visit; then go in simple confidence that God will use you. Avoid going with any set goal which you must achieve. Agendas and goals are the responsibility of the psychiatric staff. They are the ones held accountable for the patients' welfare in hospital. Occasionally you may visit a patient who acts and speaks in a confusing or strange manner. She may talk incoherently, or utter illogical nonsense. Pay your visit, show your care, but don't stay too long. Generally the nurse will guide you about how long you ought to stay. Don't be chagrined if she looks into the room or suggests you leave. Let that not keep you from coming back again for another visit.

Should you pray with a patient? I think this is suitable if you have the sensitivity to discern when it is appropriate. A depressed person may be very glad of the support and encouragement of a prayer. But let it be short. Let it express hope and invoke God's help for the patient to benefit from the therapy. You could pray for the doctors and staff too. You are a pastoral visitor, and pastoral visitors may be expected to pray when it's obviously helpful. Staff should not object.

If you find a patient who's having deep spiritual problems, by all means tell his or her pastor (who in most instances will be your own pastor). When he comes, he too no doubt will check at the nursing station for guidance. The guidance he seeks is not for theological authority, but for understanding of the patient's state of mind and emotions which will help him to know how to minister. The nurse will give a few hints as to what she feels the patient can cope with, and also what the doctor is trying to do with the person.

One final suggestion. In some hospitals there is a day-care program. Patients can stay at the hospital during the day but live in their own accommodation at night. Many patients "graduate" to day-care before they go home. Keep track of such patients at the home-end. You may also be able to take part with them in the hospital functions for day-care patients and friends, such as bingos, concerts, parties, game nights, or outings. You may also be able to re-integrate them into the congregation.

I hope that these few remarks will encourage you to visit your friends and members who are under psychiatric care, and that the hints I've given will prove helpful in this rather special kind of visiting.

14

Parish Teams And Hospital Dreams

I devote this final chapter to some dreams about ways in which the various church ministries to our hospitals could be enormously enhanced by teams of trained lay pastoral visitors. The dreams took shape as the result of a creative goal-setting technique I often use: "Wouldn't it be great if. . ." The section that deals with recruiting and training teams, however, is no dream. It is tried and tested, the product of experience, intensely down-to-earth and practical. The dream began to germinate in my mind after I had read Michael Wilson's book *The Hospital: A Place of Truth*. Wilson gives his readers a lot of good hints for the organization and deployment of clergy as hospital chaplains.

Unit Chaplains

One of Wilson's ideas, a concept practiced in Britain, is for a chaplain co-ordinator to be appointed and recognized by the hospital. This co-ordinator can be either a full-time hospital chaplain paid by the hospital or by funds from the churches, or a volunteer co-ordinator supplied part-time from the staff of a nearby parish. His task is to recruit other clergy from surrounding parishes to serve in the hospital as volunteer chaplains and so to help the churches fulfil their obligation to the sick in the community. Each of these pastors serves in a designated area of the hospital so that every ward or nursing unit has its own special chaplain. Each pastor offers this service as an outreach from the parish that he represents.

These *unit chaplains* can of course be delegates from various denominations. They are all part-timers, giving an average of from four to eight hours per week to be present on the unit. Their congregations must of necessity be willing to "lend" their pastors to the hospital for this service. It is their vicarious Good Samaritan contribution to the needy. I call it Good Samaritan because there is little promise from this ministry of any financial return to the parish. In fact it probably will cost the parish money. Neither is there any guarantee of an increase in church membership, though occasionally a grateful patient joins the church. The time spent in this ministry is time gifted to the sick in hospital. It is a sheer Inasmuch ministry, a work of love.

Over the months and years the nurses on each floor get to know their unit chaplain well. He becomes their friend. He is recognized by everyone, and hopefully a good rapport of trust and mutual help becomes established. If an emergency situation occurs on the unit at any time of night or day, the unit staff feel free to telephone their unit chaplain. If he is away or otherwise obligated, there can be an arrangement for another clergyman to be called instead. The unit chaplains "cover" for each other, just as doctors do. They can make cross-referrals to each other. Were the Baptist chaplain on Four West to find an Anglican patient wanting the sacrament of the sick, he would inform the Anglican chaplain of Two South. Most ministries such as counseling and prayer can be done by the chaplain of the unit.

The co-ordinating chaplain has to find replacements for chaplains who leave and to plan educational seminars and other events for the personal and vocational growth of participants in the ministry. It would aid him in these responsibilities to have a small committee of clergy on whose counsel he could depend. He arranges also for monthly meetings of the chaplains to iron out problems and to do business. In these meetings they deal with such matters as cost-sharing and deciding on policy matters in consultation with the hospital administration. If there is a paid chaplain, he has his own floor or two on which to minister as do all the others. His special areas might be Intensive Care and Psychiatry. He undoubtedly will also be involved in hospital working committees such as the Fire Committee, the Community Health Services Committee, or the Accident Prevention Committee, as are other middle-management personnel in the hospital. Some of his time can be spent in staff education, aiding new nurses and others to understand what the chaplains do and how they can be used, teaching them about death, dying, and grieving, and helping them to cope.

If a volunteer clergyman does the co-ordinating, he will have no time for any other hospital responsibility. Organizing the others will be enough of a job for him. He can do a little pastoral visiting just to keep his hand in, but the job of co-ordinating will definitely be enough and more for him in addition to his parish duties.

This concept is by no means a pipe dream. I once passed the idea along to the ministerial association of an Ontario town, and they made it work. This association established good liaison with the hospital administration. With the practical help of the head of the hospital's Social Service Department and some additional support from the Assistant Administrator, the system functioned so well that for some years both administration and clergy felt it served the hospital much better than any full-time paid chaplain alone possibly could. In that hospital a large framed collection of the unit chaplains' photographs hangs in a place of honor on the lobby wall, complete with the chaplains' names and the units they serve. The way the administration was involved from the start assured the success of the project. It is essential that the ministerial association, or whatever other group of concerned ministers takes up the cause, communicate continuously with administration. Let there be a two-way flow of ideas in creative dialogue at every step along the way.

Unit Lay Visiting Teams

Now suppose each unit chaplain had working with him or her a carefully screened and well-trained team of lay pastoral visitors, say, three to six for each pastor. "Wouldn't that be great?" He would have to recruit the team himself, but would not necessarily do all the training. Teams could be trained in a jointly-arranged training course. Team members could be sent back to the recruiting pastor for their internship period of pastoral visiting. They would then meet with him once every two weeks to report, evaluate, ask questions, discuss, learn, and help one another in ways that I've suggested throughout this book. Perhaps every two or three months a community-wide seminar for all the trained lay pastoral visitors could be arranged. Other special educational events could be offered for their continuing education.

These teams of lay pastoral visitors, as they served on the units over the months and years, would become as well known and trusted by the nursing staff as the unit chaplain, their pastor. A couple of team members could come with the pastor each time he visits the unit, or the lay team could take the brunt of all the visiting, referring only difficult cases and requests for sacraments to the pastor. Or he and they could apportion out the work among themselves. Lay visitors could make denominational cross-referrals too, through the unit chaplain or directly, however might be decided.

With the help of such a trained team, the unit chaplain's load could be lightened considerably. Also, the lay people would find ample opportunity to use their gifts effectively. Their ministry would be acknowledged and honored by the church. The congregation might even sponsor a Lay Ministry Sunday to honor the visitors and to hear reports of their work. The whole congregation could be involved more deeply in outreach by being asked to pray for the visitors' team on the ward, and perhaps for individual sick persons themselves. They would also pray for the whole hospital, including administration, doctors, nurses, and back-up staff. The congregations would pray not only for their own teams but for all the pastoral visitors in the hospital. And the lay pastoral visitors themselves would support one another in prayer.

One of the problems in hospitals is finding people to lead in Sunday worship. Lay pastoral visitors who have the talent could take turns leading worship every Sunday in the hospital chapel or in whatever space is provided for the purpose. Perhaps a midweek service or two, and a prayer meeting and Bible Study, could be arranged in which staff and some patients might like to be involved. The rest of the lay pastors, with the help of selected volunteers from the congregation, could bring patients who are so permitted in wheelchairs for the chapel worship. The congregations might do something special for the patients of their adopted unit on festive occasions such as Christmas and Easter. They could make or buy cards and gifts, and help the visitors distribute them. They could send flowers. They could arrange carol singing, and some kind of unit party or celebration. What a beautiful ministry to the community this would be!

The Nature Of The Team

To what shall we liken the visiting team? What kind of training is needed to do the job? Not everyone has the same concept of team effort and function. The team we want will not be like a team of horses, driven by a driver under his strict control. Neither will it be like a team of commandos in wartime, for though each individual commando is expected to use some ingenuity and flexibility in his assigned task, the procedure is carefully mapped out beforehand, and each man has definite orders. A football team of the North American type comes closer to what we're after. In the huddle the tactics are spelled out by the quarterback and the team obeys his directions, but the players actually do exercise a great deal of flexibility when the opposition interferes with the execution of the play. The best model to my mind, however, is the basketball team.

Watching such a team play you note that every member is equally important. Each one uses his skills as an individual but in fullest co-operation with all the other players. The captain of the team is out there playing too but if you don't know him you won't be able to pick him out. He plays as a peer. There's a coach on the sidelines, and he helps the captain and players to do a better job on the court. He teaches, leads in discussions about plays, works at building up team morale, and calls practice times and team meeting times for instruction and planning strategy. He's the spark that keeps the team together and in fighting spirit. Then there's all the preparation and assessment before and after every game. It is essential for the players to participate in practices and learning sessions. The more they work together, the better they'll play. The better they understand each other's strengths and weaknesses, the more they'll be able to support each other in the action and make use of the talents of each one. Also it's important to build team spirit, a spirit of co-operation and encouragement, as it is to develop individual skills and knowledge of the game.

In our team of visitors the pastor will most likely be the playing coach. Each visitor will perform his or her ministry with flexibility according to the needs of each new situation. Each will join in the team meetings for evaluation, learning, planning strategies, praying, building team spirit. They will value and understand each other, support each other's strengths, and help each other's weaknesses. They pray for one another as well as for the ministry that they're doing.

Team Recruitment and Training

How should one go about selecting and training such a team, and what arrangements should be made for coaching and team improvement? It helps if a congregation already operates on the twin principles of discerning every member's gifts and of helping individuals to get into the ministry to which God seems to be calling them. If an individual feels he'd like to take up hospital visiting, he raises the point with others in the congregation, especially with the elders and/or the pastor. They discuss the matter. All may agree about the individual's vocation or they may discern that his calling lies in another direction. Everyone should rejoice at the latter, for what more could a person want than to discover his real gifts and talents, and to hear from stable and trusted Christians the area of ministry to which God really seems to be calling him?

Recruitment may happen the other way around. The pastor in

whose church there has been little lay activity may feel, having prayed about the matter, that he himself should approach people who seem to have the gifts for this ministry, and form a team with them. However it is done, there ought to be some prayerful screening of people who come on the team.

Because I myself have to depend a great deal on the judgment of an applicant's own pastor when accepting candidates for the hospital visitors' team, I have drawn up a questionnaire. The candidate takes this to his or her minister and consults with him about the matters mentioned in it. The questions appear below. You will notice that both the candidate and the pastor are asked to sign the completed form. This arrangement is designed to bring about a serious conversation between applicant and pastor about the applicant's gifts and vocation. I interview the candidate myself also. The parish clergyman, when screening or choosing persons for the parish or unit team, might find this questionnaire a useful instrument for provoking discussion about vocation and suitability for this ministry.

Clergyman's Reference Form for Lay Pastoral Visitor

(It is expected that the prospective lay pastoral visitor will obtain his/her priest's or minister's co-operation in filling out this reference form.)

_____has asked to be involved

name

in the pastoral ministry in_____Hospital.
By carefully answering the following questions as accurately as you can you will help in determining the suitability of this person for this particular kind of ministry.

1) How long have you known the candidate?
2) What has been the nature of your association?
3) What evidence does the candidate show of emotional and mental stability?
4) (a) Have you ever entrusted someone to this person for spiritual help, consolation, or any such personal one-to-one ministry?
   With what results?
   (b) If not, *would* you?
   (c) To what kinds of people do you feel the candidate might be able to minister?

5) What personality and/or character traits do you perceive in this person that would be an asset to him/her in this ministry?
6) In what way does this person appear to be growing at this time?
7) How do you feel he/she needs to grow?
8) How does this person appear to relate to those closest to him/her?
   For example; (a) to spouse?
                 (b) to children?
                 (c) to neighbors?
                 (d) to persons in the congregation?
9) Could you briefly describe this person's apparent conception of God and of his/her relationship to God?
10) Please summarize why you recommend this person for this ministry and training.
11) Any additional comments:

Date _____

Clergyman's Signature_____

Parish_____ Phone_____

Applicant's Signature _____

Another requirement for team membership ought to be that each member take an *introductory course* in lay pastoral visitation. As I mentioned earlier, more and more courses are being offered. (This book is itself an expansion of an introductory course for lay pastoral visitors.) The prospective team members could take the course after they've been selected for the team, or the team members could be selected from among people who have already taken the course. It doesn't really seem to matter in what order the selection and the course happen, so long as both are there. There ought to be a period of practical internship for new team members. This is when it is most important to learn and use group skills, to facilitate team learning. It is also important to have a commitment from each team member. The following is an outline of the internship program I use with my own team of hospital visitors and of the commitment that the interns are expected to make.

Lay Pastoral Visitors' Team Internship

Requirements for Joining the Internship Team

1 *Introductory Course*

Each prospective member of the internship team must successfully have completed an introductory course in lay pastoral visiting.

2 *Application*

Each applicant shall submit in writing an application including :
  (i) A survey of his/her spiritual journey up to the present, current conception of God, and personal relationship to him.
  (ii) An assessment of personal strengths and weaknesses.
  (iii) Personal goals for further development of strengths and creative dealing with weaknesses.
  (iv) Reasons for believing self to be called to this ministry.
  (v) Resumé of previous pastoral experience, if any.

Note : This letter is to be shown to the applicant's clergyman to help him/her in the vocational assessment mentioned in 3 below.

3 *Clergyman's Recommendation*

Each applicant will be asked to obtain from the minister (or equivalent) of his/her church:
  (i) a clergyman's reference or "vocational assessment" using the prescribed form,
  (ii) the minister's recommendation as to her/his suitability for this ministry.

Note : Both minister and applicant must sign the reference form before the candidate sends it in.

4 *Interview with Chaplain*

Every prospective team member must agree to a personal interview with the co-ordinating chaplain.

5 *Commitments*

Each Lay Pastoral Intern will be expected to make the following commitments:
  (i) To membership on the team for twenty weeks internship, with an opportunity to join the lay pastoral visiting team as a permanent member at the end of the internship period.
  (ii) To participate in such initial orientation opportunities as may be necessary.
  (iii) To participate regularly in the twice-a-month "talk-back and learning sessions."

(iv) To visit under the direction of the co-ordinating chaplain or the parish team leader, and to be answerable to him as team leader.

(v) To do two to four hours of visiting in the hospital each week.

(vi) To join the Hospital Volunteers Association (applicable only to the chaplain's team in certain hospitals).

(vii) To agree at any time to follow the team leader's advice should it appear that the visitor's ministry lies in some other area of service than in hospital visiting. Similarly, should this be the visitor's own insight, she/he should seek the team leader's counsel about it.

(viii) To worship regularly and faithfully in his/her own congregation.

(ix) To pray faithfully for the team, the hospital, and the patients whom she/he visits.

Let us pause for a moment to summarize the various ways in which teams can be organized. I have already mentioned the *chaplain's team* that I have in my own hospital. This team works strictly under my own personal leadership and has no parish base. There could be *a visiting team working out of every congregation* in the area, visiting the people of their own membership plus any others with whom they would naturally come into contact in the course of such visitations. These parish teams need not be confined to hospital visitation only. They could call in nursing homes and private dwellings as well. A third type of team structure and operation would be *the unit team*, a group of trained lay people working with a parish based unit chaplain in that part of the hospital where he has his particular field of responsibility.

It would be an ideal arrangement for members of the unit teams to be known to the co-ordinating chaplain of the hospital, if there is one. Perhaps he could be involved in the initial screening. The introductory course on lay pastoral visiting could be given by the co-ordinating chaplain.

The Ministering Team is a Learning Team

In order for the teams to maintain interest and grow in ministerial skills, continuous learning is an absolute necessity. The scriptures encourage us to work out our salvation with fear and trembling, and to grow in every way with God's help. The team must therefore be not only a ministering team but an efficient learning team. So the team members need to learn *how* to learn together.[13]

Development of the learning team takes place by using the technique of group discussion as an instrument. When team members have become adept at free, active, and responsible participation in group discussion, they move on to learn how to plan together for their own learning needs. Needless to say, such skills are extremely useful for a group of people who want to grow not only in Christian qualities, but in Bible understanding and one-to-one visitation skills. Whenever a group of people come together to gain learning and inspiration for a task, they bring assets with them which, if put to use for the whole team, can help it greatly. There are various kinds and various grades of assets. A Christian team ought to be able to draw on them all as a means of helping others. We can summarize these assets with the acronym GRADES as follows.

Learning Assets which are present in
every group of adults (GRADES)

1 Gifts: The God-given talents and spiritual endowments which the various individuals in the group can share with each other (see Rom. 12:6, 1 Cor. 12:7, 25, 27).

2 Resources: By this is meant the varieties of information, materials, equipment, aids, and facilities that members can, when necessary, make available to the group.

3 Associates: Every group member has associations *outside* the group. These associates often can be called upon, as resource persons, to offer their knowledge and skills to the group or to make their resources available when needed.

4 Differences: Our individual differences make it *possible* for us to learn from each other and to help each other grow. They enable us to enrich each others' lives.

5 Experiences: Every individual's store of personal experiences is a source of learning for others, when shared.

6 Skills: These are acquired abilities that we can put to work to help the learning group achieve its goals.

A Note of Encouragement — "And I myself am satisfied about you, my brethren, that you yourselves are full of goodness, filled with all knowledge, and able also to instruct one another" (Rom. 15:14).

In order to activate each member's personal assets for the benefit of the group's ministry and learning, I have gathered together ten principles of adult Christian development: ten STRATAGEMS.

The Ten Principles of Adult Christian Development

1 *Sharing* in the planning for team learning.

2 *Training* for the learning team in how to learn together.

3 *Responsible* participation by every team member.

4 *Active* participation by everyone — no idle members!

5 *Techniques* which are varied and appropriate to the particular kind of learning being undertaken.

6 *Acceptance* of each other as unique persons and fellow members of Christ, despite differences.

7 *Goal setting* to give positive direction to the group's efforts, so that everyone is clear at all times as to exactly what the group is trying to do.

8 *Evaluation* of learnings by the learners themselves.

9 *Motivation* without compulsion, that is, voluntary participation.

10 *Service to others* as the spirit of the whole undertaking.

In keeping with the idea of the learning and ministering team which I have been delineating, a certain *concept of leadership* must be assumed. The team leader must have as his goal the *enabling* of all team members to do three things: (i) to enhance their gifts and skills, (ii) to improve their implementation of these for the achievement of group goals, and (iii) to help the group establish its learning goals. The leader must be able to help the team members focus their energies on the work they are doing: when it is learning, on learning; when it is ministering, on ministering. He works on the principle of *freeing* people to do what they're called to do, not on maintaining his position or prestige as leader.

Moreover, team members should learn how to support and strengthen the leader in his leadership, enhancing it as they share the responsibility of helping each other in the group's chosen tasks. They listen to each other and build upon one another's contributions. They accord one another attention and respect. No-one dominates with lengthy speeches. They help each other to say what's on their minds, to develop their ideas. They're at ease with each other, accepting even occasional silences as creative, thoughtful interludes.

They prepare ahead of time for meetings, as necessary, and help everyone to take part — like a "basketball team" on which everyone does his bit, not a regimental platoon taking orders.

It helps a great deal if the team can get together for an inaugural weekend for two purposes: to begin learning how to learn as a team, and also to grow in love, regard, and understanding of one another. The same weekend could be used to agree on group goals and on the focus and direction of the team's ministry. It could end with a service of worship and dedication to the visiting ministry.

Another helpful tool, which could be used to develop team spirit and create opportunities for sharing and learning, is a program created by Graham Tucker and Douglas Blackwell on the basis of years of trial and error in developing Christian co-operation in learning and ministry. It is described in their publication entitled *Experiencing Christian Community* (see reading list at the end of this chapter). This community-building program is set out step-by step, every step being based on some scriptural principle. Creating community, the authors acknowledge, is really the work of the Holy Spirit, but it depends on our co-operation with him and our willingness to work together at building the life and ministry of the body of Christ.

Planning Procedures

Knowing how to plan together for the team's own learning needs is another basic essential. When the whole team knows the procedures, much heat and confusion can be avoided, and some very practical and relevant learning plans can be produced. Experience has shown that the following procedure, if followed carefully, will result in a sensible plan in the shortest time. I have incorporated the steps into seven questions: Who? What? When? Where? Why? How? and Then?

Who?   The first important question to answer is, "For whom is this learning program being created?" The answer must be based upon an understanding of the circumstances, background, culture, values, beliefs, and problems of the learning community. When the learning experience is being planned for the group itself, the answer to Who is fairly easy. A little more thought is required when the program is being prepared for a prospective audience.

What?   What are the sorts of things that will help the prospective learners? Start by noting down several broad areas of need and interest. Then narrow them down to one. After that, think of all the headings that ought to be dealt with under this broad area of interest and need. You'll have to narrow things down again to the most necessary ones at the moment.

When? Fix your dates and times. The available time makes a difference to how much you can accomplish. If you seem to need several sessions to cover what you've decided on under What, you can plan on that. You may have to go back and revise the What a little, too.

Where? This really ought to be dealt with along with all the previous questions. The space available, and type of accommodation makes a difference. If you have a choice of locales you are lucky!

(By now I can almost hear someone saying, "What a lot of fuss and bother!" My only reply is that if you try it, you'll see the value. Best of all, this systematic way of planning will help you save time and make your learning programs much more varied and interesting. Use the procedures even when planning for a few people. It works for groups of four to eight as well as for crowds of hundreds.)

Why? This is the question so many people forget. No wonder they get snarled up and bogged down! And no wonder their teaching-learning programs seem to lead nowhere in particular. Under Why, you clearly state the purpose of the learning event and its goals or hoped-for outcome.

How? Before we can actually say how the program will be done, we need to know what *resources* are available to use in learning what we need and to achieve our learning goals. We need also to choose the appropriate *educational techniques* that will make best use of the resources. The resources may be people, films, audio-visual aids, books, records, cassettes, models, or displays. The techniques might be speeches, panels, role-plays, skits, debates, group discussion, demonstrations, and so on. Many books are available to enrich the learning group's repertoire of possible techniques. Finally, the *program schedule* is drawn up by deciding which resources to use out of all those that are available, and selecting the best means to use them for the purpose of the particular learning event. In summary:

> > (a) list available resources.
> > (b) list possible techniques.
> > (c) draw up the program outline.

Then?   This is another much neglected question. After we've put
        on the program and carried out our learning plan, we
        evaluate it together. The team goes over the learnings, the
        results, the changes which have taken place, the ways
        they've benefitted and grown, the advantages which the
        clients or patients have received as a result of the learning
        achieved in the program. The planning is also evaluated for
        its strengths and weaknesses. This whole evaluation effort
        in itself becomes a learning process. It helps the learning
        team to know how things might better be done next time. It
        helps the team become a better learning and planning team.

Combined with prayer and commitment this entire operation is
offered to God as a reasonable service motivated by his Spirit. The
team members are built up and God is glorified. The local congregation begins thus to live up to its Christian obligation to reach out to
the needy. It becomes a training camp of the kingdom, not merely in
word and doctrine but in deed and in power.

Recommended Reading

Understanding People And Their Needs

Bachmann, Charles. *Ministering To The Grief Sufferer.* Fortress, 1964.

Brandt, Catharine. *Forgotten People.* Moody, 1978.

Brown, J. Paul. *Counseling With Senior Citizens.* Fortress, 1964.

Frankl, Viktor. *Man's Search For Meaning.* Pocket Books, 1959.

Glasser, William. *Reality Therapy.* Harper and Row 1965.

Gray, Robert M., and Moberg, David O. *The Church And The Older Person.* Eerdmans, 1977.

Hand, Samuel E. *Adult Education: A Review Of Physiological and Psychological Changes In Aging And Their Implications For Teachers Of Adults.* State Department of Education, Florida, 1965.

Harris, Thomas. *I'm O.K. You're O.K.* Spire, 1967.

Havinghurst, Robert J. *Human Development And Education.* Longmans Green, 1953.

Hessel, Dieter, ed. *Maggie Kuhn On Aging.* Westminster, 1977.

Howe, Reuel. *The Miracle Of Dialogue.* Seabury, 1963. *The Creative Years.* Seabury, 1959.

Jones, Rochelle *The Other Generation.* Spectrum, Prentice-Hall, 1977.

Kavanaugh, Robert. *Facing Death.* Penguin, 1972.

Kubler-Ross, Elisabeth. *On Death and Dying.* MacMillan, 1969.

Nouwen, Henri J.M. *Aging.* Image, Doubleday, 1976.

Selye, Hans. *Stress Without Distress.* Lippincott, 1974.

Tournier, Paul. *The Violence Inside.* S.C.M., 1978.

Westberg, Granger. *Good Grief.* Fortress Press, 1962.

The Practice Of Ministry

Clinebell, Howard.   *Basic Types Of Pastoral Counseling.*
                          Abingdon, 1966.
Dicks, Russell.   *Principles And Practices Of Pastoral*
                          Care. Fortress Press, 1963.
Hiltner, Seward.   *Pastoral Counseling.* Abingdon, 1949.
Keith-Lucas, Alan.   *Giving And Taking Help.* University Of
                          North Carolina Press, 1972.
Kennedy, Eugene.   *On Becoming A Counselor.* Seabury,
                          1977.
McNutt, Francis.   *Healing.* Ave Maria Press, 1974.
Scherzer, Carl J.   *Ministering To The Physically Sick.* For-
                          tress Press, 1968.

Team Learning

Bergevin, Paul and   *Participation Training For Adult Educa-*
McKinley, John.   *tion.* Bethany Press, 1965.
Bergevin, Paul,
Morris, Dwight, and   *Adult Education Procedures.* Seabury,
Smith, Robert.   1963.
Stone, Howard W.   *The Caring Church (A Guide For Lay Pastoral*
                          Care). Harper and Row, 1983.
Bergevin, Paul, and   *Design For Adult Education In The*
McKinley, John.   *Church.* Seabury, 1958.
Tucker, Graham H. and   *Experiencing Christian Community.*
Blackwell, Douglas C.   Aurora Conference Centre, Aurora,
                          Ontario.

The Hospital Situation

Crichton, Michael.   *Five Patients — The Hospital Explained.*
                          Knopf, 1970.
Herrman, Nina.   *Go Out In Joy.* Pocket Books, 1977.
Wilson, Michael.   *The Hospital: A Place Of Truth.* Univer-
                          sity of Birmingham, 1971.

The Spiritual Perspective

Frankl, Viktor.   *The Unconscious God.* Simon and
                          Schuster, 1975.
Howe, Reuel.   *Man's Need And God's Action.* Seabury,
                          1953.
Lewis, C.S.   *The Problem of Pain.* Geoffrey Bles,
                          1940.
Yancey, Philip.   *Where Is God When It Hurts?* Zonder-
                          van, 1977.

Notes

1 Such courses are offered at Wycliffe College, Toronto; St. Michael's Hospital, Toronto; York Central Hospital, Richmond Hill; Oshawa General Hospital; and in the Anglican Deaneries of Parkdale, Saint James, and Scarborough in the Diocese of Toronto.

2 One parish with an excellent practical and academic lay pastoral training program is the Laos School of Theology with headquarters in Emmanuel Anglican Church, Richvale.

3 The idea for this list came from Philip Yancey's description of a series of visitors in his award-winning book *Where is God When it Hurts?*

4 The first three of these needs of the patient are basic assumptions in Dr William Glasser's psychiatric approach called *Reality Therapy.*

5 *Man's Search for Meaning.*

6 *The Problem of Pain* by C.S. Lewis is a classic book on the subject, along with *Where is God When it Hurts* by Philip Yancey.

7 Students of Cabot and Dicks will recognize the source of some of these thoughts.

8 One helping resource I have often used is THEOS *(They Help Each Other Spiritually),* a fellowship of widowed persons that can be a tremendous support to a bereaved spouse. Canadian address: Trinity Presbyterian Church, 2737 Bayview Avenue, Willowdale, Ontario.

9 In *Exploring the Psycho-Social Therapies through the Personalities of Effective Therapists,* a report for the United States Department of Health, Education, and Welfare, James Dent concludes that neurotic clients are definitely not well served by people who try to solve their problems.

10 *On Death and Dying.*

11 From an article by Dr Bruce Johnson in the *United Church Observer*, June 1974.

12 Irene Mortenson Burnside in *Nursing and the Aged*, page 25.

13 One of the best instruments I know to help a team of people learn how to learn together is the Indiana Plan for Adult Education in the Church. Short courses are given in the Adult Education Department of Indiana University, Bloomington, Indiana.

Index